MW01221728

The rights of Stephen Murga.. , _ _.. Donald G. Simpson to be identified as the editors of this work have been asserted according to the U.S. Copyright, Designs and Patent Act of 1988 and appropriate Canadian copyright law. The rights to be identified as authors of materials in this collection of work have been asserted according to the U.S. Copyright, Designs and Patent Act of 1988 and appropriate Canadian copyright law.

Printed in the United States of America.

Murgatroyd, Stephen 1950-
Simpson, Donald G. 1934-

Renaissance Leadership and The Renaissance Way
ISBN 978-1-300-78937-6

Dedicated To

All in the Innovation Expedition Network and Renaissance Leaders Worldwide who have supported The Renaissance Way Since 1992.

We challenged each other to live our lives as Renaissance Leaders – engaging and inspiring others to lead change with passion and foresight. This book will give you the insights, ideas and frameworks to do the same.

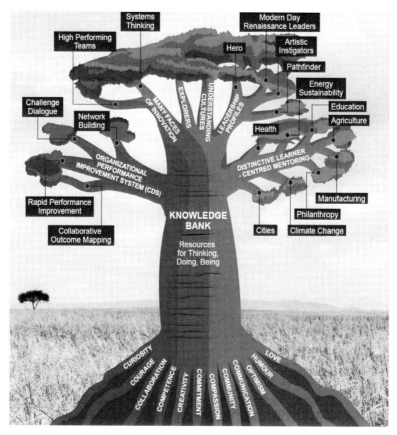

The labels in the image, reading around the tree:

Systems Thinking
High Performing Teams
Modern Day Renaissance Leaders
Hero
Artistic Instigators
Pathfinder
Energy Sustainability
Challenge Dialogue
Network Building
Education
Agriculture
Health
MANY FACES OF INNOVATION
EXPLORERS
UNDERSTANDING CULTURES
LEADERSHIP PROFILES
ORGANIZATIONAL PERFORMANCE IMPROVEMENT SYSTEM (CDS)
DISTINCTIVE LEARNER - CENTRED MENTORING
Rapid Performance Improvement
Manufacturing
Collaborative Outcome Mapping
KNOWLEDGE BANK
Resources for Thinking, Doing, Being
Philanthropy
Cities
Climate Change

Roots: CURIOSITY, COURAGE, COLLABORATION, COMPETENCE, CREATIVITY, COMMITMENT, COMPASSION, COMMUNITY, COMMUNICATION, OPTIMISM, HUMOUR, LOVE

Image developed by Leah Andrew for Don Simpson.

The cover image for this book is a Baobab Tree ("the Tree of Life") – common across Africa and parts of Australia. .

The Baobab Tree is revered for offering shelter and sustenance to diverse species and for maintaining ecological balance. It symbolizes the resilience of individuals and communities in changing circumstances. It is an appropriate symbol describing the nature and purpose of *The Renaissance Way*.

TABLE OF CONTENTS

PREFACE

This is a revised edition of *Renaissance Leadership – Leading and Rethinking the Future*, first published in 2011. The first edition is out of print but is still available as an e-book. It is a fitting time for a new edition with substantial new material. Don Simpson, co-author, celebrated his 90th birthday in July 2024 and has been awarded the Order of Canada in recognition of his lifetime work as an Imagineer and systems innovator.

Don developed the thinking behind this work during his time as a Vice President at the Banff Centre for the Arts, beginning in 1990. In this, he was joined by Stephen who was then Dean of the Faculty of Administrative Studies (later the Faculty of Business) at Athabasca University. Both institutions were Alberta based – then a hotbed of technological and environmentally related innovation.

For over three decades, members of The Renaissance Way network (formerly known as The Innovation Expedition) have been working to accelerate innovation, spur growth and create jobs, encourage a strong focus on health and wellbeing through compassion and care and have been making a difference to organizations and communities.

Each year since 2011, MBA students at Athabasca University have been exploring the ideas contained here. They not only critically examined the leadership framework presented here but sought out and interviewed individuals around the world who embodied the framework. Interviewees ranged from the leader of the largest online retailers in the world, one of the founders of Blackberry who went on to lead a range of innovation initiatives, a nurse leader, a Grand Chief, several non-profit leaders, leaders in the arts community and a Nobel prize winner.

Their work has kept the thinking fresh. We also used this framework in a pioneering leadership development offered to potential leaders within Conoco Phillips Canada. The program was an intense, project-based learning program where teams were set challenging, real-world corporate problems to solve. They were asked to leverage the Renaissance Leadership framework to do so. Creative talents were unleashed, specific problems evident within the corporation were solved and the organization became one of the best places to work in Canada. This was followed by a shorter development at the University of Toronto's Faculty of Medicine where a four-module program in translational research was offered, led by Don Simpson.

In mentoring, coaching, consulting and teaching, both authors have fully leveraged the framework and underlying principles outlined here to inform major initiatives for many of the Fortune 500 large corporations, non-profit organizations, small and medium-sized enterprises, healthcare organizations and arts organizations.

In the early 1990s, Don organized expeditions to major leadership events in Europe and Japan to raise awareness of the emerging Canadian network and its thinking. The aim was to build new relationships with international groups which shared similar strategic intentions and values.

This work has also stimulated international gatherings. Most recently, Stephen Murgatroyd shared the framework and its implications in a major conference on the future of leadership held in Mauritius, Africa in 2024. Abdullah Saleh, CEO of ICChange and a renaissance leader, uses the thinking and approach in his work as Director of the Office of Global Surgery at the University of Alberta and Keith Jones and Tom Ogaranko, co-founders of the Challenge Dialogue System® (CDS) Network, have been training and certifying colleagues in the use of CDS both as a technical system for engaging in important and inspired conversations, but also as a lifestyle.

This work did not begin with the publication of the original edition of Renaissance Leadership. It has its roots in Don Simpson's life journey, which began in 1958 with his founding efforts with the African Students Foundation and Crossroads Africa. His work in the 1990s with his time at the Banff Centre as a Vice President for leadership education and learning cemented his lifelong learning. In 1992, the International Institute for Innovation (the Triple I) was launched from the Banff Centre as a way of gathering ideas, materials and people together from around the world who shared a set of values and understanding of what was needed for inspired and engaged leadership in a fast-changing knowledge economy.

In 1994, Don Simpson exited the Banff Centre and joined a new start-up company called Axia NetMedia (later Axia), inspired by the vision of Axia's founder, Art Price. In 1998, he was joined by Stephen Murgatroyd, who had left his position as professor and former Dean of the Faculty of Business at Athabasca University. Axia bought Lifeskills International Ltd. and their spin-off company, Citizen Connect in 1999 and Stephen Murgatroyd became CEO of these UK based companies. In 2000, the Innovation Expedition Ltd. was created as a way of maintaining the momentum of the innovation expedition outside of the Lifeskills family of companies. Don Simpson and Dawn Ralph led this start-up organization. The Lifeskills team and Innovation Expedition collaborated on a range of initiatives and projects for the next several years. Axia sold Lifeskills International Ltd. in 2003 and Stephen Murgatroyd returned to Canada.

In 2008-9, Don Simpson was asked to teach on the Advanced Management Programme (AMP) at the Said Business School, Oxford. A hundred- and twenty-two-page outline of the thinking and rationale for Renaissance Leadership was written by Don Simpson and Stephen Murgatroyd with the considerable support from Jan Simpson (Red Oaks Consulting), who sadly is no longer with us. Called a *Travel Guide* – a key rucksack requirement of any expedition – this was the first fully documented statement about modern day Renaissance Leadership but also the dynamics of The Renaissance Way (TRW). Participants in the AMP engaged, explored, examined and extended the ideas it contained. These materials formed the basis of the 2011 first edition and also informed the MBA elective course developed at the same time which was offered 2010-2024. During this time, 450 graduate students have systematically explored the Renaissance Way.

The Renaissance Leadership book "kicked off" a series of books which explored the ideas and thinking of The Renaissance Way. These include:

- Murgatroyd, S. (2010) *Rethinking the future – Six patterns shaping the new renaissance. futureTHINK* Press | Lulu Press.
- Murgatroyd, S. (2011) *Rethinking education – Learning and the new*

renaissance. futureTHINK Press | Lulu Press.

- Knight, A. (2012). Rethinking corporate social responsibility – If only we ran the planet like a shop.
- Couture, J-C. & Murgatroyd, S. [editors] (2012). *Rethinking school leadership – Creating a great school for all students. futureTHINK* Press | Lulu Press.
- Simpson, D.G. & Murgatroyd, S. (2012). *Rethinking Innovation - Driving Dramatic Improvements in Organizational Performance Through Focused Innovation. futureTHINK* Press | Lulu Press.
- Couture, J-C. & Murgatroyd, S. [editors] (2013). *Rethinking equity – Creating a great school for all students. futureTHINK* Press | Lulu Press.
- Tully, J. & Murgatroyd, S. (2012). *Rethinking post-secondary education - Why universities and colleges need to change & what change could look like. futureTHINK* Press | Lulu Press.
- Murgatroyd, S. (2015). *How to rethink the future. futureTHINK* Press | Lulu Press.
- Aris, S.J. & Murgatroyd, S. (2017) *Beyond resilience – From mastery to mystery: A workbook for personal mastery and transformation. futureTHINK* Press | Lulu Press.
- Murgatroyd, S. (2023). *Being courageous – The skills of courage. futureTHINK* Press | Lulu Press.

Don Simpson also began an epic journey: capturing his life's work and the work of the innovation expedition in a series of fourteen logbooks – over 5,000+ pages of text – which aim not just to chronicle the journey but tease out and share insights and understanding from seventy years of work, coupled with insights from those encountered along the way. Quite the journey, but one openly shared with hundreds of fellow travelers who collaboratively wished to pursue The Renaissance Way.

The work was more than just writing. It involved mentoring, consulting, innovating, creating, connecting, collaborating, engaging, exploring, failing and falling, reimaging and re-engaging. This new edition updates the thinking about leadership and has many additional components that were to be found in the 2011 edition.

In particular, the new thrust of the team behind this work is to move from a focus on Renaissance Leadership to a broader focus on a Renaissance Way as a way of being in organizations, communities and networks. The idea here is simple: how can we use the characteristics of Renaissance Leaders to live fuller, more meaningful lives and, in doing so, contribute to social good and well-being? As the world becomes more complex, anxiety-laden and difficult to navigate, trusted Renaissance Leaders will be in high demand.

A part of this focus has been on integrating artistic ways of knowing, being, sharing and understanding with all aspects of life. We continue to give emphasis to balancing thinking skills with doing skills and the skills of being.

This is captured in the simple idea: "an artist at every table." If a musician, sculpturer, actor, writer, landscape artist, poet, games designer, animator was sitting with us right now, what would they share and how would this change what we say, think and do? This idea informed the thinking of the innovation expedition network from its origins at the Banff Centre and continues to do so through work we did on the Artistic Olympics and the Arts Games with Sylvia Sweeney and the work that continues with the team of Artistic Instigators. Indeed, salons held in Harbour Square in Toronto often mix artists with others, which always leads to new and creative outcomes. This has led to some significant developments at the Blackhurst Cultural Centre, founded by Itah Sadu, on the site of the iconic "Honest Ed's Emporium."

The Renaissance Way
The Renaissance Way is a highly flexible, globally tested, comprehensive and integrated leadership development approach. It has been designed to mentor leaders in building a high capacity for collaborating and unleashing innovations to successfully address complex tasks in order to:

- Drive transformational changes that dramatically improve organizational performance

- Promote cross-cultural harmony

- Stimulate sustainable development in one's own community and in others around the world

This process integrates the best creative altruism found in the non-profit and social enterprise sectors, along with some best examples of creative entrepreneurship in business. It also integrates the work we have been engaged in since we began working together in the 1990s.

This Book

Our work on this book has been helped by comments, contributions and insights from a variety of members of this network. In particular, the late Jan Simpson (Redoaks Consulting), the late Bob Church, Herbert Wong, Gay Haskins, Doug James, Michele Johnson, Bernadette Conraths (WHU, Koblenz) and Matthias Kipping (Schulich Business School, York University), Keith Jones and Tom Ogaranko (Challenge Dialogue Systems), James Orbinski (Master, Massey College), Tom Jackson (actor and entrepreneur), Abdullah Saleh (iChange and the Centre for Global Surgery at the University of Alberta), Brenda Kennedy (Kennedy Consulting), Leah Andrew (Andrew-Perry) and others. They have each made many helpful suggestions which have influenced this work. Dawn Ralph, Susan Wasson, Carlos Algandona and the late Michelle Baker have also provided invaluable practical support.

Others are now pursuing the strategic intentions of the Renaissance Way and doing so with purpose and vigour. Eric Beynon, for example, has used his life-long commitment to environmental sustainability to test the construct that change can be incentivized through challenge-based prizes. He was closely involved in the X-Prize as a designer and assessor and more recently in Prince William's Earthshot Prize as a competitor – the team he worked with (Advanced Thermovoltaic Systems – developers of a completely new end environmentally friendly turbine). We have been promoting this challenge-based approach to change for over twenty years.

We have always said that "you cannot cross a chasm in two small leaps" – but it certainly helps to know how wide the chasm is before you jump!

Let the journey continue!

Stephen Murgatroyd, PhD FBPsS FRSA and D.G. Simpson, PhD CM
For The Renaissance Way
January 2025

The citation for Don Simpson's Order of Canada reads:

> Don Simpson has demonstrated a lifetime commitment to innovative leadership development and cross-cultural engagement. Throughout a career spanning seven decades, he has been an academic, entrepreneur, researcher, program designer, administrator and mentor, working and residing in various communities around the world. He founded the Innovation Expedition and the Renaissance Expedition, bringing together creative, collaborative, compassionate innovators committed to changing the world for the better.

The logbooks detail every aspect of this journey. This book presents the "essence" of the Renaissance Way and the key features of Renaissance Leadership. Our hope is that it will inspire you to choose to live and practice the Renaissance Way — making a difference to the lives, experiences and possibilities for others.

Stephen Murgatroyd, PhD FBPsS FRSA
Bowen Island, July 2024

CHAPTER 1: THE CONTEXT FOR LEADERSHIP

"We desperately need more leaders who are committed to courageous, wholehearted leadership and who are self-aware enough to lead from their hearts, rather than unevolved leaders who lead from hurt and fear."
Brené Brown *Dare to Lead* (2018)

Introduction

Leadership is about becoming, personal mastery, and being more of yourself. It is, as Warren Bennis once observed, "as simple as that, and it is also that difficult." It is about courage, determination, compassion, care, and connection. It is increasingly about living and working with uncertainty, ambiguity, and paradox. Today, leaders need to be champions of their organization's purpose – what the organization stands for and what impact it seeks to have. They need to show courage in enabling all in the organization to deliver that purpose and their potential every day. They need to show skill in enabling this to happen. They have to "muddle through" complex, demanding and strange times to make happen what needs to happen.

This work of leadership, which has always been demanding, is becoming more difficult and challenging no matter what kind of organization one works in. Complexity and ambiguities grow as change accelerates and this brings with it fear, uncertainty and a sense of risk. Not only is the world VUCA (volatile, uncertain, complex and ambiguous), but it is also BANI (brittle, anxiety-making, non-linear and, for many, incomprehensible), with new fractures and discontents occurring almost daily.

As society becomes more complex, more multi-cultural, and more fractured, leaders are at the "sharp end" of what our VUCA | BANI world does to the psychological (and therefore psycho-physical and psycho-social) well-being of individuals, communities and organizations. Leaders are increasingly seen as the trusted source of truth and as guides to the future. They are expected to be Renaissance Leaders, whether they know it or not.

1

Let us look at just one example: healthcare. In healthcare leaders and their teams face growing challenges of rapidly increasing demand for service, especially in relation to the core presenting conditions of stress, anxiety, depression, suicidal thoughts, bipolar disorder, schizophrenia and children with exceptionalities and also newer conditions such as climate eco-anxiety and solastalgia, prolonged grief disorder and, in North America in particular, a growing number presenting with "delusion-like-beliefs" (DLBs) – culturally sanctioned and shared beliefs based on conspiracy and lies resulting in psychological distress. As demand for service increases, available resources to support this work in most jurisdictions – skilled and effective clinicians, support staff, and finance – are getting scarcer. Leaders are under tremendous pressure, resulting in less satisfying engagement levels between leaders and clinicians, amongst clinicians and between clinicians and their patients, as well as increased pressure on all to "perform." These challenges create complex relationship issues within the team and create the conditions in which staff experience moral distress. When coupled with growing levels of bureaucracy and accountability and the growing complexity within health and care systems caused by mass immigration, leadership is becoming more complex and challenging.

If these challenges were not enough, healthcare organizations in Canada, the UK, the USA and many other countries are constantly re-organizing, rightsizing, reshaping and redefining what they do, how they are organized and adding new public assurance and certification requirements to already complex systems.

Some of the complexity leaders of organizations that deal directly with people in need are caused by the self-inflicted volatile and uncertain change management activities of health executives and political entities, most of which fail. It is not surprising, therefore, that it is increasingly difficult to recruit and retain courageous, innovative leaders.

It is the same for education systems, government organizations, non-profit corporations and for-profit corporations. Finding, developing and retaining leaders who can lead complex organizations and are able to respond to threat, challenge, change and opportunity is becoming increasingly difficult.

2

At the same time, organizations are changing. Patterns of work have changed post-pandemic, with more people working from home and several organizations adopting a 4-day week. Workplaces are increasingly multigenerational – home to Baby Boomers, Generations X, Z, Alpha and Millennials. Artificial intelligence and other technologies are changing how we work and who we work with. Supply chains have become more vulnerable to disruption either from extreme weather events, civil unrest and war or from emerging technologies. As Yogi Berra used to say, "the future isn't what it used to be!"

Patterns and Developments

Our work on anticipatory governance and futures thinking requires us to track a number of patterns, trends and developments which impact people, communities and organizations. For the last two decades, we have tracked these specific developments so as to better understand the context in which leaders have to think, feel and act. We do not see this work as about predicting the future but as about developing scenarios and an understanding of possibilities, probabilities and challenges. The key patterns we track are:

1. **Environment:** Climate change and the attempts to mitigate climate change impacts. More specifically, what actions can be taken to impact both the rate and depth of change climate change will produce. We have worked on issues in health, agriculture, forestry, supply chains, space, population and transport with this lens in mind.

2. **Demography:** Patterns of birth, life and death are changing. Birth rates are falling around the world (especially in developed economies) and people are living longer. When taken together, these two developments are leading to severe skill shortages around the world. This in turn has led to higher levels of immigration (both legal and illegal) and more complex communities. Globally, it is now expected that the global population will not reach the peak many anticipated before the pandemic. It is now estimated that there will be app. 11 billion people by 2100 – up from the 8.1 billion in 2024.

3. **Technology:** Emerging technologies – ranging from AI and quantum computing to new building materials, new uses of forest products, new

3

technologies for agriculture and food production, new health technologies.

4. **Debt**: Growing levels of personal, corporate and government debt and the way this shapes leader activity in a range of organizations. This also involves an understanding of risk and uncertainty.

5. **Trust**: A sharp decline over the last twenty years in the trust between individuals and those who lead and inform them. It is now the case that business leaders are amongst the most trusted sources for truth across the world.

6. **Identity**: Changes in the way in which individuals and communities understand their own identity and that of others. This manifests itself in a variety of ways but is seen most clearly in inter-generational workforces where different generations see themselves and the place of work about their self very differently. It is also seen in new patterns of work and the strong focus, especially in younger workers, on securing work-life balance.

7. **Fractured Politics and the Growth of Populism**: Political reality impacts the work of all organizations, as those facing up to the consequences of elections in France, US, UK, Italy, Hungary, Japan and elsewhere can attest. More populist, right-of-centre politicians, some with extreme views about minorities or proven-wrong views on economic growth and development (e.g. faith in trickle-down economics), are now in power, and there is a growing use of power and authority to govern rather than collaboration and consensus.

8. **Shape Shifting Global Economy**: The new middle class and markets are in Asia, Africa and India. Over half of the $1 billion corporations are now headquartered in Asia, and this continent has most of the fastest-growing cities in the world. As Africa, India, and Asia develop, North America, Europe, and Latin America struggle to secure economic growth. This seismic shift in economic focus is significant and has an impact on the flow of goods and services and the futures for highly qualified people. This will now be deeply impacted by the

growing isolationist economic strategy being pursued by the US government.

There are many sub-patterns and trends related to these eight major shifts, but these provide a strong context for understanding the challenges of leadership.

Disrupting the Flow of Certainty

All of these patterns are trends, are disruptive and can lead to disruptive events. The impact of disruptive events on our perception of stability is deeply rooted in cognitive processes. According to Event Segmentation Theory[1], our brains constantly create and update mental models of ongoing events to predict future outcomes. When disruptive events occur, they challenge these models, leading to increased prediction errors and forcing our cognitive systems to reset and adapt. This process of constantly updating and readjusting alters our sense of perceptual constancy, making the world seem less stable and predictable. As a result, individuals may experience a heightened state of alertness and uncertainty, affecting decision-making processes and long-term planning. Some find the growing uncertainty of the modern world difficult to cope with. It is one explanation many demographers offer for declining rates of fertility.

In the economic sphere, income volatility has emerged as a significant disruptive force, eroding the sense of financial stability for many individuals, communities and organizations. Research shows that experiencing income volatility is linked to poorer financial planning decisions and a lower internal locus of control. This shift in perceived control over economic fate can have far-reaching consequences, affecting not only financial behaviours but also overall well-being, health and life satisfaction.

The rapid pace of technological advancement is also creating new challenges

---

[1] See Zacks, Jeffrey M., Nicole K. Speer, Khena M. Swallow, Todd S. Braver, and Jeremy R. Reynolds. 2007. "Event Perception: A Mind-Brain Perspective." *Psychological Bulletin* 133(2):273–93. doi: 10.1037/0033-2909.133.2.273.

5

to global stability, revolutionizing various sectors from education, retail, travel and healthcare. These emerging technologies are outpacing the development of institutional frameworks and governance structures, leading to a dangerous gap in local, organizational, national and global governance and exacerbating feelings of unpredictability and instability on a societal level. This puts immense pressure on leaders to anticipate the future, act locally, and immediately to ready their organizations for constant change.

The cumulative effect of these disruptive events is a fundamental transformation in how we approach stability and predictability. Traditional models of risk assessment and long-term planning are becoming increasingly obsolete in the face of rapid, unpredictable changes. This new reality demands a shift towards more flexible, adaptive strategies that can withstand and even thrive in conditions of uncertainty. Organizations and individuals alike are being forced to develop new competencies in agility, resilience, and continuous learning to navigate this ever-changing landscape. As we move forward, the ability to embrace uncertainty and adapt quickly to disruptive events will likely become a critical factor in personal, organizational, and societal success.

Agile, Adaptive, Compassion Leaders – The Renaissance Way
Faced with pressure to improve performance at a time of uncertainty, lower costs, increase impacts, and manage the dynamics of a multigenerational team, what is a leader to do? Given the VUCA | BANI nature of the world in which they operate, what can leaders do to equip themselves for the rapidly changing world?

In response to the pressure to adopt leadership "best practices" and foster innovation, leaders need to be agile, adaptive, and responsive to local conditions and circumstances. Being agile and responsive is the key to improving performance and surviving in an uncertain, brittle, and ambiguous world. This requires leaders to show:

> **Compassion and Empathy** - agile leaders exhibit compassion by acknowledging other people's perspectives, giving them the care they

need to meet their work and personal goals, involving them in decisions where appropriate, and building a sense of partnership and community within their teams. This compassion leads to higher engagement, more trust, and stronger relationships with team members and stakeholders.

Transparency and Openness - agile leaders foster a culture of transparency by being emotionally transparent themselves – they practice personal mastery (Murgatroyd & Simpson, 2010). This creates environments of trust where team members feel empowered to share more of themselves, leading to deeper trust and more empathetic, compassionate leader-team relationships. Transparency also helps mitigate the perception of ambiguity as threatening and prevents team members from interpreting a lack of full disclosure as "social rejection."

Empowerment and Autonomy - agile leaders recognize that people work best when they are enabled, engaged, and energized. Empowering individuals is a key skill of the agile leader, as is "running interference" so as to enable them to work with excessive oversight. Agile workplaces thrive when individuals and teams are empowered to own their work. Leaders should offer a powerful statement of the purpose of the work and the organization, create a framework for them to operate and then let their people decide how to achieve those outcomes. Too much "command and control" produces too few outstanding outcomes.

Adaptability and Flexibility - agile leaders must be adaptable and flexible and adjust their actions and behaviours as circumstances change. Among the most important elements for success is their desire and ability to learn from experience paired with changes in the environment and then use that learning to perform well in new situations. Agile leaders encourage teams to experiment with new ways of working, quickly test new ideas, and refine them over time. In this work, they strive to move from Stage 4 in Kegan's developmental stage to Stage 5.

7

Continuous Learning and Improvement - agile leaders have a strong focus on developing people and a passion for learning. They encourage regular feedback loops, emphasize the importance of data-driven decision-making and experimentation, and foster a culture of continuous learning through training, workshops, and knowledge-sharing. Providing learning opportunities helps sustain team motivation while encouraging open discussion of important issues. They also practice cross-boundary learning by exploring ideas, practices and research in fields other than their own.

Courage and Passion - Courage enables leaders to take calculated risks, challenge the status quo, and make difficult decisions when necessary. It allows them to stand up for their beliefs and values, even in the face of adversity or uncertainty. Conversely, passion fuels the leader's drive and commitment to their work and the people they serve. It inspires and motivates team members to strive for excellence and fosters a sense of purpose and meaning in their work.

These six characteristics, in turn, require the leader to be a systems thinker – to understand systems dynamics and interaction to better anticipate consequences and challenges. It also requires them to connect and understand what is happening in other parts of the world and how their peers in Canada, Australia, New Zealand, the USA and elsewhere have tackled the issue they find challenging. Thinking globally to strengthen actions locally (thinking "glocal") is a vital capability that is evident in agile leaders.

Implicit here is that Renaissance Leaders living the Renaissance Way are optimists who often use humour and imaginative responses to challenging situations. In troubling times, such as the time that this book is being written, the promotion of a sense of optimism "has become a duty not just a casual indulgence."

The underlying principle of this view of leadership in a VUCA | BANI world is that leaders should practice what Africans call "Ubuntu": "I am because we are" as opposed to "I think. Therefore, I am!" The term reminds us of our shared humanity and the importance of treating mental health issues not as individual failings but as part of the broader human experience that we must face together with compassion. It also reminds leaders that there is no leadership without followership, which ultimately depends on purpose, passion, courage, trust, and compassion. This chapter has described the underlying features of a new renaissance in leadership, which is practiced by leaders worldwide in health, business, arts and non-profit organizations. The balance of this book elaborates this basic thinking, describing the eight characteristics of Renaissance Leaders, the importance of courage and learning from failure and the need to practice what are called the 7Cs (curiosity, creativity, collaboration, commitment, courage, competence and compassion). We will also describe what it is like to live as a leader using the Renaissance Way as their mantra and frame for their work and interactions with others.

CHAPTER 2: THE EIGHT PRACTICES OF RENAISSANCE LEADERS

Introduction

The *Innovation Expedition* has been working with leaders in government, for profit and non-profit organizations across the world for close to forty years. We have leveraged this experience and that of our highly experienced network to ask the question: When we look at the "stand out" leaders of the current age — those who understand the new renaissance and are leading their organizations to be best in class — what do we see them doing?

The Eight Practices

Our response is that there are a great many factors which shape effective leadership within a sector or organization, but that eight key characteristics stand out as necessary conditions for Renaissance Leadership. We studied other leadership models, as you will see, and reviewed the thirty-six dominant leadership competencies which we found dominated the literature. We reflected on what this meant for our view of leaders in these renaissance times. In our view, Renaissance Leaders:

Practice personal mastery

They have high integrity and view self- awareness as a prerequisite for leadership. They work hard to develop their capacity to innovate, and to inspire others to join them in making the world a better place.

Apply a glocal mindset

They have a keen sense of history and seek a holistic understanding of changes taking place on a global scale. They use this global perspective as they address local challenges and seize opportunities (global and local — hence "glocal").

Accelerate cross-boundary learning

They constantly seek to satisfy an intense curiosity about every facet of human life, past and present, scientific and artistic, technical and social. They guide others in distilling meaning from a morass of information and efficiently apply their learning in creative ways to nurture innovation and drive improved performance.

Think back from the future

They are readily able to imagine and articulate alternate futures and work back from there – connecting with lessons from the past to better understand the present and choose among possible paths to the future they see.

Lead systemic change

They are systems thinkers who seek out patterns, inter connections and interdependencies. They are skilled in seeking common ground and nurturing productive collaboration across diverse parts of a system – be it an organization, a sector, a community, a network – to solve complex problems and drive largescale change.

Drive performance with a passion

They care that their leadership makes a substantive and sustainable difference and are relentless in their commitment to performance. They articulate clear (and high) expectations of themselves and others, create focused strategies for innovating to achieve these ends, and are disciplined about assessing progress.

Demonstrate courage

They are unafraid to be bold, creative, direct and innovative in seeking change and performance and have learned to learn from failure.

Instinctively use Ubuntu as a powerful way of being

"Ubuntu" is an African term for understanding that individuals are successful because of the collective efforts of those with whom they work: "I am because we are" is the guiding idea.

Expanding the Practices

These eight characteristics are not listed in order of importance nor are they intended to be complete – it is the list we have arrived at on this stage of our expedition. In the first edition of this book, we listed six characteristics (1-6 above). It became clear, especially during and after the pandemic, that two additional characteristics were needed: courage and Ubuntu.

The pages which follow provide more detail and examples of each of these six characteristics and suggest some activities which you can pursue to deepen your understanding of each of them. The intention is to lay out the terrain and suggest some map references which will ground your journey to understanding the new renaissance and its emerging leaders.

These ideas were developed and refined through a series of workshops at the Saïd School of Business, Oxford with mature international leaders and have been refined in dialogue with many organizations and individuals since. Many have found this a powerful and effective starting point for a conversation about leadership in a 21st century organization exactly as we intended. They have also been explored by over 500 MBA students at Athabasca University for over a decade, involving each student undertaking an in-depth interview with an individual they consider to be a renaissance leader.

Some have observed that the key characteristics of Renaissance Leaders, as described in more detail in the balance of this book, are deceptively simple to list but difficult to practice daily. Others have suggested that keeping the list of characteristics close to hand helps them be better leaders daily. Our intent, in offering this thinking, is to challenge you to think about a simple question: "What kind of leadership does a renaissance organization lead and how can the key characteristics of these leaders best be captured?"

CHAPTER 3: PERSONAL MASTERY

Introduction

Renaissance Leaders practice personal mastery: they have high integrity and view self-awareness as a prerequisite for leadership. They work hard to develop their capacity to innovate, and to inspire others to join them in making the world a better place. Here are some of the things that are indicative of the search for personal mastery:

Approaching life as artwork in progress: For aspiring leaders or students of organizations coming of age in North America in the 90s, the phrase "personal mastery" is indelibly associated with Peter Senge's seminal book, *The Fifth Discipline: The Art & Practice of the Learning Organization* – one of the five core disciplines essential to building organizations "where people continually expand their capacity to create the results they truly desire, where new and expansive patterns of thinking are developed and nurtured, where collective aspiration is set free, and where people are continually learning how to learn together." For Senge, personal mastery goes beyond competence and skills, although it is grounded in competence and skills. It goes beyond spiritual unfolding or opening, although it requires spiritual growth. It means approaching one's life as a creative work – a work always in progress.

Making the analogy with a master craftsperson whose personal and professional proficiency enables the best pots or fabrics to emerge from the workshop, Senge describes personal mastery as a lifelong process of approaching life as an artist would approach a work of art. The keys are continually clarifying what's important to you, learning how to see current reality more clearly, and working with the forces of change to resolve the creative tension between your vision of what might be and where things are now.

People who practice personal mastery are acutely aware of their ignorance and their incompetence, but also deeply self-confident.

Asking the right questions to manage oneself: The notion that deep self-
-awareness is the foundation on which a leader's ability to act effectively
in the world is not new. The admonition "know thyself" is said to have
been carved onto the walls of the temple of Apollo at Delphi, greeting
leaders coming to consult the Oracle on matters of war and state in ancient
times. What is new, according to Peter Drucker, writing in the 1970s, is that to
have even a chance of success and achievement in the new economy,
knowledge workers need to learn to manage themselves. Until sometime in
the mid-20th century, the norm was for people to be born into a line of work,
and so knowing your strengths was irrelevant. If the peasant's son wasn't
good at being a peasant, he failed.

Now people have choices. They have to discover what they're good at.
Whereas through most of history, most people have been subordinates
who did as they were told, knowledge workers must answer a new question:
"What should my contribution be?" To successfully make that contribution,
they must understand their personal mode of performance, and pay attention
to the strengths, values, and performance modes of others. We each need to
create our own learning and development pathway and see learning and
growth as a cornerstone of effective leadership.

Renaissance Leaders, in addition to developing a sense of personal
mastery, manage themselves – they are self-starters and capable of
undertaking complex projects without losing their sense of self or being
"taken over" by the projects and their demands – in the midst of complexity,
Renaissance Leaders are an island of simplicity: they understand the
complex, but can make clear and explicit what needs to be done, by whom,
by when and they know what part they must play in making things happen.
Knowing themselves and how they work best enables them to manage and
support others.

Exploring diversity: There are, of course, many systems designed to help
people appreciate such differences. One can trace a link from the work of
the Greek doctor Hippocrates (460-370 BC) on how bodily fluids or
"humours" (blood, yellow bile, black bile and phlegm) affected human

behavior to the variations on the sanguine, choleric, melancholic and phlegmatic personality types described by 20th century psychologists. These days, people are most likely to explore the differences through tests based on the Myers-Briggs Type Indicator or the True Colors character cards, which one can now explore via a website dedicated to this work.

Some may find themselves drawn to Peter Koestenbaum's Leadership Diamond Model, originally conceived by Herbert Wong. It is a three-dimensional model for probing the mysteries of life and leadership by asking you to reflect on your fundamental orientation towards the world – exploring and understanding your way of being intelligent: are you a visionary, a pragmatist, a people person, or an explorer?

Your fundamental mastery of the different modes of existence – your way of being competent: your mastery of greatness (maintaining excitement and hope), of polarity (managing uncertainty and coping with ambiguity), of resistance (your openness to the truth about yourself), of teaching (leading by helping others learn).

Your levels of depth (forms of enrichment) – your level of professional enrichment (personal or individual development), of social/cultural/ethnic enrichment (societal context and community), psychological enrichment (the unconscious as a source of both power and failure), and philosophical enrichment (questions of consciousness, spirituality).

Much more of our exploration and use of Human Dynamics can be found in the Logbooks of the Chief Explorer, Don Simpson. There he explains just how influential this work and his experience of working with the Human Dynamics team was.

The framework that Peter Senge found most useful is Human Dynamics, created by Dr. Sandra Seagal and David Horne. In the foreword to their 1997 book, Senge writes:

"One of the foundational strengths of Human Dynamics…is that the differences among the personality dynamics are truly a source of richness to be celebrated and appreciated, without any implicit judgment…the Human Dynamics approach is inherently developmental. Rather than sticking people in a box and saying, "This is how you are," it illuminates our distinctive patterns of growth and change. Each personality dynamic is seen as a whole system, evolving in particular ways…It leads to seeing each of us as a process rather than a thing."

Human Dynamics is based on the premise that three fundamental aspects of human functioning combine in highly specific ways in people to form distinct patterns of functioning called "personality dynamics". These three patterns are shown below in Figure 1.

Mental	Thinking – Objectivity – Vision – Overview – Structure – Values
Emotional	Feeling – Subjectivity Communication – Organization – Create Imagination
Physical	Making – Doing – Actualizing – Sensory Experience – Practicality – Systematic Experience

Figure 1: Patterns of Functioning

While the interaction of these three patterns (also referred to as principles) creates nine potential dynamics, five occur most commonly (see stories on following pages). Understanding these patterns gives us unique insights into how we -and others -experience our environment, process information, prefer to communicate, learn, problem solve, relate to ourselves and others, maintain wellness and develop. Each type brings unique and essential gifts.

Human Dynamics seeks to "illuminate our different ways of functioning so we may make more efficient and enlightened use of ourselves." Just as important, we can also then work consciously to meet the needs of people with other personality dynamics, recognizing that "diversity is the intended purpose of nature – to be respected, celebrated, and utilized."

Human Dynamics' developmental thrust starts with understanding and fully realizing the gifts inherent in our foundational dynamic (the name of which reflects the two patterns with which we are most at home – mental, emotional, and physical). But the third pattern is always present in each of us, and the richer journey that so excited Senge is the development and integration of this third strand.

To illustrate the power of these ideas, here are some extracts of stories from five combinations of principle factors for five different people. As you read these, put yourself in the position of someone who works with them – what would be your challenges in working with this person?

Mental – Physical: "I am most attuned to the world of thoughts, vision, concepts, and overviews. I am easily able to maintain focus and can inspire that gift in others. I often bring structure, objectivity, and precision to projects and interactions…I seek to articulate overarching principles and values to which all can subscribe."

Emotional – Objective (Mental): "I am a problem solver with an affinity for generating new ideas and promoting innovation. I relish change and challenge and am alert for windows of opportunity…striving to cultivate group synergy for the purpose of building something new and enduring that will benefit humankind.

Emotional – Subjective (Emotional): "All of my experiences are personalized. I have personal responses to everything and want to connect personally with everything and everyone. I have a wide range of feelings and am sensitive to and interested in the feelings of others...I have a visionary capacity, which can enable me to be an inspirational communicator and an effective long range 'seer.'"

Physical – Mental: "I am a natural systems thinker interested in concrete work. I want to translate thoughts and ideas into practical results that satisfy a need or solve a problem. I especially excel in the tactical implementation of work...Another deep purpose is to create unity out of diversity by maintaining bonds among all group members in the spirit of community."

Physical – Emotional: "I am practical, detailed, thorough, and precise. I am also a natural strategic planner and systems thinker. I have a strategy for almost everything I do. I tend to assemble and reassemble data until interconnected patterns or systems change...One of my deep purposes is to formulate and implement plans and activities that reflect a compassionate concern for the welfare of people and that answer a collective need."

The underlying idea of this work and thinking is that there is a need to find the relationship between thinking, doing and being: integrating the various features of we think, feel, do and reflect into a focused person able to respond well to challenge, change and opportunities.

Examples of Leadership Derailers

Here are six examples of the in which leaders own thinking or behaviours can impair leadership performance:

- When self-confidence slides into arrogance, leaders become blind to how their actions are hurting themselves and their organizations.
- Charisma and an appropriate leader-like "presence" can become melodrama, detracting from other people's performances and impairing ability to see what's going on.
- Prudent thoroughness turned into excessive caution and over-analysis can result in a fatal failure to act decisively at a critical moment
- Healthy skepticism can become habitual distrust, leading employees to watch their backs rather than their work, and stop believing in themselves
- A willingness to challenge the status quo and redefine industries can degenerate into impulsive mischievousness and destructive rule-breaking
- An appropriate perfectionism taken too far can mean the little things are put right while the big things go wrong

And so on. The book is written through the lens of the leader because the authors believe that the vast majority of top executives don't receive adequate feedback or confrontation to help them understand their personalities and their impact they have on others or the organization as a whole. But leaders of any stripe can benefit from understanding their personal derailers, figuring out what kind of stress triggers them, and learning to manage these stressors proactively.

Seeking support

While personal mastery is, by definition, focused on an individual leader, it need not be solitary.

Most Renaissance Leaders seek help from others to maintain personal mastery – coaching, guidance, mentoring, as well as opportunities for challenges that will stretch their skills, network and imagination.

More and more, virtual networks are becoming part of the mix as people use technology to build a web of support and knowledge that can span the world. Blogs and shared bookmarking, member driven news sites like diigo.com, popular social networks My Space and Facebook, and professional networks such as LinkedIn – the Internet offers a wealth of opportunities for people to seek advice and specialized resources, learn and share learning. There are also a growing number of dedicated sharing and exploration spaces around key topics that preoccupy leaders.

In our own work we have developed over many years a Global Mentoring Team (GMT) and have made several attempts to create a Global Intelligence System (GIS). Both are needed, though experience tells us that they are difficult to create,

CHAPTER 4: APPLYING A "GLOCAL" MINDSET

Introduction
The term "glocal" refers to the idea of understanding the global context in which local actions need to be taken and the impact local actions could have on global developments.

"The world is flat," proclaimed Thomas Friedman in 2005, more than 500 years after Christopher Columbus ostensibly championed the idea of a spherical earth to a skeptical world (in fact the concept is at least as old as the ancient Greeks and was generally accepted by scholars and navigators in 15th century Europe).

Friedman's world is flat in the sense that globalization has leveled the competitive playing fields between industrial and emerging market economies. The global web of information and communication technologies has made it possible for companies to locate call centers thousands of miles from the customers they support, outsource accounting and programming to offshore contractors, create complex global supply chains that take advantage of the most cost-effective sources of skilled labour wherever they may be located. The collapse of the Berlin wall and the end of the cold war marked the beginning of a new economic openness to the world on the part of countries like Brazil, India, China and Russia – countries that are now such significant players on the world markets that they have their own acronym: BRIC.

With competitive advantage now driven more by innovation – the creation and application of knowledge – than by availability of raw materials and cheap electricity, location matters less. While people are migrating from less-developed economies to fill the gap created by declining birth rates and aging populations in the more developed countries in North America and Europe, countries like India are putting their highly educated knowledge workers to work on virtual global teams without ever leaving home. Financial capital now flows freely around the globe. Increased competition and shifting trade patterns are disrupting industries, and challenging key and established notions about statehood and economic boundaries.

Exploring the new world of the global knowledge economy

Renaissance Leaders understand that a new world has been emerging over the past four or five decades, and that navigating it will require fundamental adjustments to their mental maps. Just as physical maps of the world are influenced by one's biases – North American maps routinely put North America in the centre, even at the cost of splitting Asia in two, while Chinese maps clearly show "the middle kingdom" in its rightful place – so too do our assumptions about the way the world works influence what we are able to see. We offer as a starting point the 21 axioms above, capturing what we see as some of the salient features of the global knowledge economy.

Global management practice

While Drucker asserts that the global knowledge economy rests on foundations developed in the Western world – Western science, tools and technology, production, economics; Western-style finance and banking – Ronald Lessen as early as the late '80s was attempting to present a framework for global management that encompasses management theory and practice from around the world. Positing four domains of management, he explores how different cultures have predominant attractions to different domains. He's interested in how left-brain/right-brain research and the Oriental concept of Ying/Yang are both contributing to a growing tendency to integrate across domains. He notes the Japanese concept of mutual interest gradually appearing in Western leadership and organizational theory, traditionally dominated by self-interest.

Four Global Management Domains

- **Primal:** Focus on the basics; concern for the tangible and for people; generating pride, enthusiasm and love
- **Rational:** Focus on effective management of resources, converting capabilities into results
- **Developmental:** Products and markets evolve in stages; collaboration overtakes competition
- **Metaphysical:** Focus on the flow, velocity, quality and quantity of energy; drawing from both ancient wisdom and modern physics

Globality

According to Harold Sirkin, James Hemerling and Arindam Bhattachara, in the new global reality we will all eventually be competing or collaborating with everyone from everywhere for everything. The successful companies will be continually scanning the world for competitors, potential partners and new ideas. They will be doing business in ways that bring together the best practices and strategies developed over centuries in the Occidental and Oriental worlds. In their book *Globality*, they tell the remarkable stories of companies that achieved worldwide success, suggesting that we might soon be recognizing that:

- The fastest growing global brands are Goodbaby, Embraer, Tata, BYD, Cemex, Bharat Forge
- The most celebrated business leaders are Wang Chuanfu, Lorenzo Zambrano and Anand Mahindra
- Your daughter's first choice for an MBA just might be Skolkovo Business School outside Moscow
- Your next favourite car could be a snappy new Dongfeng

The Renaissance City

The phrase "think globally, act locally," originally associated with the environmental movement, is now widely applied to the challenge of effective action in the face of overwhelming complexity and interconnection. While nothing is now purely local – with every local action both influenced by and influencing broader global forces – local action is the antidote to the paralysis that could take hold from too intense contemplation of the full global picture.

The locus of economic and creative activity in the Italian Renaissance was the city-state – Florence initially, but by the early 16th century Venice and Rome. Today, as capital and ideas flow freely across national boundaries, the spotlight is once again being put on the role of cities in driving innovation and wealth-creation. It is in cities that we find the critical mass of diverse perspectives, knowledge, and skills that produces innovation: technological and social innovation, innovation in products and services, innovation in how work gets done and institutions are designed and managed.

We said earlier that at a country level, location now matters less. Some have posited that since the Internet, modern telecommunication and transportation systems have made it no longer necessary for people who work together to be together, "place" has no importance in the knowledge economy. Richard Florida counters this "geography is dead" myth by noting:

> Not only do people remain highly concentrated, but the economy itself — the high-tech, knowledge-based and creative-content industries that drive so much of economic growth — continues to concentrate in specific places from Austin and Silicon Valley to New York City and Hollywood, just as the automobile industry once concentrated in Detroit. Students of urban and regional growth from Robert Park and Jane Jacobs to Wilbur Thompson have long pointed to the role of places as incubators of creativity, innovation and new industries (Rise of the Creative Class, p.219).

The difference, according to Florida, is that the cradles of the new economy are not thriving for such traditional economic reasons as access to natural resources, transportation routes, tax breaks or business incentives, but rather because creative people want to live there. The companies then follow the people — or, in many cases, are started by them. Creative centers provide the integrated eco-system or habitat where all forms of creativity — artistic and cultural, technological and economic — can take root and flourish (p. 218).

Arguing in *The Rise of the Creative Class* that nearly half of all wage and salary income in the US is now generated by what he calls "the creative class" — scientists, engineers, artists, musicians, designers and knowledge-based professionals — Florida suggests that the key challenge for cities that aspire to be economic winners in the new economy is understanding what attracts creative people to a place. In our terms, they need to recognize the characteristics of a Renaissance City.

Florida explores the interrelated set of factors that work together to create a "quality of place," attractive to creative people:

- **What's there:** The combination of the built environment and the natural environment; a proper setting for the pursuit of creative lives.

- **Who's there:** The diverse kinds of people, interacting and providing cues that anyone can plug into and make a life in that community.

- **What's going on:** The vibrancy of street life, café culture, arts, music, and people engaging in outdoor activities – altogether a lot of active, exciting, creative endeavors.

One of the things that attracts talent to a city is multiple career opportunities in their field. As Florida notes in his reference to Hollywood and Silicon Valley, while the world is flat in the sense that interconnectivity has begun to level the playing field, it is also "lumpy." Centres of excellence stand out against the flat landscape – Mumbai for technology, London for financial services, Silicon Valley for high tech industry. These are places where clusters of like-minded firms have grouped together to build a powerful business community – competing and collaborating in turn and spawning the creation of support services and infrastructure.

Local action for global change

Under "leading systemic change," we explore Margaret Wheatley's work on how new understandings in the scientific world can provide new insight into organizations. She further suggests that quantum perceptions of reality may help us understand why thinking globally and acting locally is exactly the right approach. Acting locally – working with the system you can get your arms around – has always been considered a sound strategy for changing large systems. Newtonian science would say that each local act creates incremental change, and "little by little, system by system, we develop enough momentum to affect the larger society."

But if you take the quantum view that space everywhere is filled with fields – "invisible, non-material structures that are the basic substance of the universe," then you might imagine that:

> These changes in small places, however, create large systems change, not because they build one upon the other, but because they

share in the unbroken wholeness that has united them all along. Our activities in one part of the whole create non-local causes that emerge far from us. There is value in working with the system any place it manifests because unseen connections will create effects at a distance, in places we never thought. This model of change - of small starts, surprises, unseen connections, quantum leaps - matches our experience more closely than our favored models of incremental change.

CHAPTER 5: ACCELERATING CROSS BOUNDARY LEARNING

We have seen, and will see elsewhere in this journey, how exposure to discoveries in one discipline opens up new lines of thinking and innovation in another – the application of scientific exploration of systems thinking and quantum physics to business and how we understand organizations, for example. Peter Drucker, in several of his writings, has pointed out that the changes that affect a body of knowledge most profoundly do not, as a rule come out of its own domain. For example, "After Gutenberg first used moveable type; there was practically no change in the craft of printing for 400 years – until the steam engine came in."

The Italian Renaissance saw breakthroughs in every aspect of human endeavour: in architecture and biology, painting and astronomy, cartography and medicine, literature and chemistry, sculpture and political economy. Perhaps this explosion of innovation was at least in part attributable to a sense that the rigid barriers had not yet gone up between the professional disciplines. Key players in one field were often players or influencers in another. Young people were not streamed into either art or science early in their education. Intuition and reason could be spoken of in the same breath. Renaissance Florence did not take the view that engineers were by definition illiterate, and artists incapable of running anything.

Our Definition of Innovation:

> "A process for extracting economic and social value from knowledge. Putting ideas, knowledge and technologies to work in a manner that brings about a significant improvement in performance".

It has become an axiom of the global knowledge economy that the ability to learn and innovate faster and better than the competition is now the key to sustaining competitive advantage and success. In this context, the notion of what learning means and how it's done well is being richly explored. Learning no longer conjures up the image of the youth apprenticed to a trade (or the tasks of household management) for six or seven years then applying the learning without much variation beyond gradual improvement in proficiency for the rest of his or her life. We've moved beyond the idea that learning means children in neat classroom rows being drilled in reading, writing, and 'rithmetic. We now talk of lifelong learning, learning organizations, action learning, and agile learning. As the Internet makes information on every imaginable topic widely available across the globe, we also worry about how to make sense of it all – make meaning, turn data into knowledge, then manage that knowledge.

Canada, our home and a major focus for our work on innovation, is not doing well at innovation. It is strong on invention – developing ideas and new science and creating protected intellectual property but is weak at running these inventions into products or services which earn sustained revenues. Despite several attempts by governments, investor groups and networks of inventors, Canada is slipping down the global innovation and competitive league tables. New thinking will be required to shake up the innovation system and that thinking will require a greater understanding of collaborative risk taking and markets.

We need to adapt the view that innovation is a rigorous process that can both be understood and replicated. What is more, in our view, it can also be taught and practiced with the support of effective innovation coaches and mentors/

Learning is work/work is learning

If the truly unique contribution of management in the 20th century was the 50-fold increase in the productivity of the manufacturing worker, according to Drucker the most important management challenge for the 21st century is how to increase the productivity of knowledge work and the knowledge worker. If knowledge work is fundamentally about the creation and application of ideas, then the implication is that learning is a new form of labour. Far from being something that requires time out from engaging in productive activity, it is at the heart of productive activity.

This concept is at the core of approaches like "action learning," codified by Kolb and others starting in the 1970s. The continued popularity of action-learning approaches reflects the failure of conventional leadership development to translate into practical increases in organizational performance. While it is highly useful to take individuals out of their daily routine periodically to be exposed to new ideas and receive intense coaching, this in itself will not create effective leaders. Leaders return to their organizational context without necessarily having developed the skills to translate their individual learning to organizational learning, to apply it to practical problems, to use it proactively to drive innovation.

Action learning approaches tend to assume that the starting point of learning for most adults is experiencing/doing. They treat the workplace as the classroom and real-life problems as the learning vehicles. The Galileo Educational Network, for example, has been using action learning – something now generally referred to as "authentic learning tasks" – as a basis for inspiring children in classrooms across North America, with great success (see www.galileo.org).

Amongst the first action research projects undertaken at the Banff Centre by Don and his team explored the construct of "the learning organization" and what it meant to key leaders across a range of business sectors. The findings of this work informed a great deal of the early stages of the Renaissance Leadership work and the creation of the innovation expedition.

More important and recent developments have included short and intense learning experiences – boot camps, month long challenges, flexible micro-learning – all aimed at connecting emerging leaders with like-minded colleagues who then work together in flexible ways to solve their own challenges and real-world problems, like food waste, loneliness, eldercare. The Royal Society of Arts (RSA), based in London, is leveraging its fellowship network for just this purpose, using two frameworks (design thinking and regenerative thinking) to shape solutions, Colleagues "learn as you go" so as to make significant advances possible.

Learning with the whole brain

A popular book published in the late 1970s was Betty Edwards' Drawing on the Right Side of the Brain, which claimed that anyone with sufficient ability to thread a needle or catch a baseball could learn to draw – not necessarily become a great master but develop an acceptable competence. Far from being a magical ability possessed by only a few:

> "The magical mystery of drawing ability seems to be, in part at least, an ability to make a shift in brain state to a different mode of seeing/perceiving. When you see in the special way in which experienced artists see, then you can draw....My aim is to provide the means for releasing that potential, for gaining access at a conscious level to your inventive, intuitive, imaginative powers that may have been largely untapped by our verbal, technological culture and educational system...From this experience you will develop your ability to perceive things freshly in their totality, to see underlying patterns and possibilities for new combinations. Creative solutions to problems, whether personal or professional, will be accessible through new modes of thinking and new ways of using the power of your brain" (pp. 3, 56).

We have said that multi-disciplinary learning is important because innovation so often happens when ideas from divergent knowledge domains come together in novel ways. But multi-disciplinary learners are also much more likely to be exercising different parts of their brain, to be accessing their whole intelligence. Howard Gardner has posited the importance of becoming adept in applying a range of different "intelligence." He suggests seven, but we have reduced them here to six:

1. **Verbal linguistic intelligence** – involving a sensitivity to the meaning, order, sounds and rhythms of words and the functions and powers of language.

2. **Musical intelligence** – the ability to "hear" music in one's mind, to compose and to think musically, especially in terms of melody and rhythm.

3. **Logical-mathematical intelligence** – the ability to use reasoning, ordering and logical thought for problem solving, whether in mathematics and science or in the ordinary affairs of life.

32

4. **Visual-spatial intelligence** – including the ability to perceive accurately, to visualize and to create artistic transformations of the visual word.

5. **Bodily-kinesthetic intelligence** – as exemplified in people like dancers and athletes who develop unusual mastery over the motions of the body.

6. **The personal intelligences** – including two aspects: The ability to access one's own inner feelings and the ability to understand and be able to relate to other people.

Making Meaning

In the days when each manuscript was painstakingly written and illuminated by hand, access to information beyond one's small local sphere was a luxury available to very few. Today, as the internet has made the explosion of available information triggered by the printing press look puny by comparison, the learning challenge is not so much finding information as making meaning and creating knowledge.

There are a variety of ways to think about this challenge. At the most tactical level, organizations are thinking about knowledge management systems that provide ready access to the collective memory of the organization to all within it, in a practical, useable format. The best of such systems is technology enabled, driven by a very clear view of why the system is being created and how it will be used.

At a more strategic level, Renaissance Leaders are thinking about how to distill the essence of meaning from masses of information, and communicate it to others in a simple, impactful way. Systems thinking and the kind of recognition of frequently recurring patterns we discuss in that section play a role here. Given that the telling and hearing of stories has been central to how cultures define themselves and create community for as long as there has been language, it's not surprising that the language of literature often creeps into the dialogue about how to make meaning. Ikujiro Nonaka writes in an HBR article in the early 90's about how Japanese companies drew on metaphors and similes to focus the collective knowledge of teams around a product or service challenge: If the automobile were an organism, how would it evolve? If we thought of the drum of a copy machine as a beer can – which costs very little to manufacture – where would that lead us? Storytelling has emerged as an essential leadership capability in the drive to understand and apply cross boundary learning.

This work – and it is demanding – requires Renaissance Leaders to integrate their thinking and action into a coherent and focused way of being. That is, all can see that what they say is what they do and what they mean.

CHAPTER 6: THINKING BACK FROM THE FUTURE

In *Beyond Certainty: A Personal Odyssey*, Charles Handy recalls the liberating moment when he realized the one message he'd taken away from all his schooling was not only crippling but wrong. That message was that every major problem in life had already been solved, and the aim of education was to transfer the answers from the teacher to him. The realization that this was not true, he says, changed his life:

> *The world is not an unsolved puzzle, waiting for the occasional genius to unlock its secrets. The world, or most of it, is an empty space waiting to be filled.... I did not have to wait and watch for the puzzles to be solved; I could jump into the space myself. I was free to try out my ideas, invent my own scenarios, create my own futures. Life, work, and organization could become a self-fulfilling prophecy, with my making the prophecies... (p. 17).*

Most definitions of leadership incorporate the notion that leaders create and articulate a compelling vision that inspires their followers: They see the long view, paint a concrete picture of a desired future, effectively communicate and manage the dream. For Renaissance Leaders, putting their lively imaginations to work on exploring possible futures and using what they find there to guide their actions in the present is both second nature and a finely honed skill. Renaissance Leaders can imagine and articulate what an organization needs to be 10-20 years "out" from the current reality and have a sense of direction and a pathway to get back from the future to now.

Notice that we don't say *have a plan to move from now to the future*, but a plan to *get back from the future to now*. It's a crucial difference. Given that the future isn't a straight line from the present, there is a need to fully understand the stages of *development through which the organization will have to pass working backwards from the future. These stages may look very different from those that might be developed if you worked from now to the future.*

Beyond the rear-view mirror

Historically, organizations have managed largely through a rear-view mirror, relying heavily on measures of past performance to plan the future. They have focused on "lag indicators" – looking back – as opposed to "lead indicators" – predictive measures of the future. Using lag indicators often implies that we know the way in which these shape the performance of an organization, a market or a system. But if the future is different from the present, lag indicators are often measures of an old way of working, not the new.

More and more, companies are investing in identifying and learning how to use predictive indictors – such as shifts in customer perception of the value a business offers versus its competitors, or leading economic indicators such as housing starts, retail price index or GDP growth. Only a few regularly supplement this past/present view of the world with a disciplined approach to exploring possible futures, looking for risks and opportunities.

Consider this proposition. Given how rapidly and constantly the global knowledge economy is changing, many of today's schoolchildren will find themselves working in jobs that don't yet exist, creating products that have not yet been imagined. A teacher looking at education through a rearview mirror might complain that students today are hyperactive, have short attention spans, no discipline and no respect – worse, they actually treat teachers as their equals!

A teacher imagining a future in which core competencies include systems thinking, a lively curiosity, a global mindset, an ability to collaborate, multitask and understand nonlinear approaches might watch a student at a computer through a different lens. Perhaps these children are in fact developing strong foundational skills for future success as visualization specialists, web gardeners, tacit knowledge catchers, nanofabricators, robot trainers, wind finders, bio-informationalists – or Renaissance Leaders? Working back from the future provides a radically different perspective on the same behaviour than the one we see if we look just from the present.

Take another example. There is a growing shortage of fresh water in the world at the same time that the demand for water is increasing. Mexico, for example, is currently extracting a great deal of its freshwater from aquifers, reducing the potential of future supply. Saudi Arabia has water for another ten years or so and then faces real difficulty. If we imagine a future where all water has to be imported into a country and water usage has to be curtailed, we can quickly see how different a plan this would be from one in which we looked at current demand and supply levels and sought simply to increase water use efficiency. We can also envisage social unrest over water supply (Nairobi already had a water riot in July 2007), especially where access to water is based on wealth, not need. Smart money is moving to new technologies for desalination, water reuse and recycling, and water control.

Rehearsing the future

Conventional wisdom in the early 1970s held that the price of oil would stay stable. When it rose suddenly and dramatically in the mid70s in the wake of what became known in the Western world as "the oil crisis," Royal Dutch/Shell was already prepared to drastically change its business in response. They had already "rehearsed" this future. Borrowing techniques employed in military planning in World War II, Pierre Wack and his colleagues had developed a tool for preparing the company to deal with a variety of possible futures, putting a strong focus on imagining futures that were not widely expected to happen. What became known as "scenario planning" rejects the idea of the future as a straight-line extrapolation of current trends, considering instead the broad range of forces shaping the local and global environments and the alternate futures they might drive.

Such scenario planning is again in use today, as most analysts predict oil will reach $200 a barrel by 2015 and stay at or above that price. The impact on all of our lives will be substantial. The impact on transport and food costs was already apparent when oil was at around $130/barrel. Renaissance Leaders are already imagining a future very different from the present – one in which alternative means of communication, new food sources, and new methods of food distribution are occurring. New retail forms and new global supply chains will also be created.

As a tool and a discipline, scenario planning exhibits the Renaissance tendency to cross discipline boundaries and integrate left and right brain thinking. While scenario planning may have been born in the military, it draws heavily on the world of literature. Peter Schwartz, examining the history and practice of scenario planning in *The Art of the Long View*, states:

> *"It is a common belief that serious information should appear in tables, graphs, numbers, or at least sober scholarly language. But important questions about the future are usually too complex or imprecise for the conventional languages of business and science. Instead, we use the language of stories and myths. Stories have a psychological impact that graphs and equations lack. Stories are about meaning; they help explain why things happen in a certain way. They give order and meaning to events — a crucial aspect of understanding future possibilities.... They open people to multiple perspectives, because they allow them to describe how different characters see in events the meaning of those events. Moreover, stories help people cope with complexity "(pp. 4041).*

Scenarios provide a way of having a conversation about the future — giving shape and meaning and creating frameworks for a dialogue. More significantly, they can provide a basis for analyzing trends and information and building models. A great deal of our understanding of climate change comes from just such work.

But scenario planning is only one tool of strategic foresight. There are others. Key amongst them is understanding potential discontinuity — the disruptive power of some new development, especially a new technology or new patterns of social behaviour.

When the Internet began to be widely available in 199394, few imagined it would radically change the way in which the world works. But it has. The music industry, financial services and the travel industry have all faced major changes in how they operate. In the case of the music industry, the Internet has led to the collapse of traditional ways of buying and selling music, as well as the creation of new supply chains and new patterns of consumer behaviour.

With wireless broadband technology becoming more powerful and widely available, and digital devices – not just computers, but Internet enabled handheld devices – capable of receiving information and data at very high speeds, we can expect more disruptions, most especially in education, health and financial services.

Creating the future

"...vision without systems thinking ends up painting lovely pictures of the future with no deep understanding of the forces that must be mastered to move from here to there."

Peter Senge, *The Fifth Discipline* (p. 12)

Critiques of scenario planning argue that too often it becomes an esoteric exercise that may create interesting stories but rarely leads to productive change in organizations. Renaissance Leaders have developed the skill of connecting their imagined futures with deep learning from the past to guide their choices in the present. Systematically looking at the future while at the same time developing an understanding of history of a particular issue, idea, opportunity or region enables Renaissance Leaders to ground their thinking in time and space.

"Strategic foresight" has emerged as a useful discipline in this regard. Fusing "futures" methods such as scenario planning with strategic management, strategic foresight stresses that the point of visiting the future in your imagination is to use what you see to chart the most successful course toward it – to detect adverse conditions, guide policy, shape strategy, explore new markets/products/services.

Strategic Foresight: A Definition

This is a simple definition of strategic foresight, one commonly used by teachers of the discipline:

> "the general ability to create and maintain a high quality, coherent and functional forward view, and to use insights arising in useful organizational ways"

This definition leads practitioners to undertake three different kinds of foresight work:

- **Pragmatic foresight** – aimed at carrying out tomorrow's business better by seeking to be systematic about understanding the future

- **Progressive foresight** – going beyond conventional thinking and practices and reformulating processes, products and services using quite different assumptions so as to position the organization as ahead of the competition or first to act in the light of changing conditions

- **Civilizational foresight** – that seeks to understand the aspects of the next civilization to which a community or region is moving – for example, Zimbabwe twenty years from now.

The primary methods of strategic foresight are:

- **Scenario Planning and Review** – using a variety of methods for exploring the factors that may shape the scenario

- **Trend Analysis, modified for certain risks** – a form of scenario planning using hard data to look at "what if?"

- **Uncertainty Analysis** – that looks at the disruptive and likely events that will change how an activity is being undertaken. These can be statistical models, historically based observations or speculative. This is also known as "What If Analysis"

- **Risk Analysis** – that uses the rigorous processes now associated with risk analysis to look at the likely outcomes of a process

- **Delphi Process** – that uses experts (potentially in large numbers) in a rigorous process for soliciting responses to key ideas and placing them in order of importance

- **Challenge Dialogue System**™ – a systematic, template driven process for engaging a community of interest (e.g. a cross section of leaders associated with the fibre industry sector worldwide) – we say more about this in a subsequent chapter.

- **Back-Casting / Historical Analysis** – Looking from the future back. For example, offering the Annual Report of the Alberta Chamber of Resources for 2025 and seeing what issues this raises

- **Transformative Cycle** – developed by Richard Slaughter and others in Australia, this uses a set of models of change to identify the patterns of change within an industry (the industry S curve) and then looks at where a particular technology is in relation to that cycle (the T-cycle). For example, Ray Kurzweil provides an analysis of the speed at which information processing technologies are replaced, which in turn provides a basis for understanding the future of the data industry and the needed development and investment patterns

- **Causal Layered Analysis** – developed by Sohail Inayatullah (a leading futurist and coeditor of the *Journal of Future Studies*), this method uses a variety of different approaches (layers of understanding) to understand in depth the drivers for different future scenarios. UNESCO has used this method to look at educational systems and literacy. Some countries have used it to look at the future of health systems

All of these methods rely on: (a) an ability to access thought leaders in the chosen area of work and to explore with them their understanding of the current situation (a test of their reality) as well as their understanding of what is likely to happen over the next 20-40 years; (b) an ability to access the most reliable, current and verifiable data about the performance and trends within a sector – e.g. biotechnology; (c) the ability to work in a workshop mode to develop scenarios that may involve individuals "suspending" current beliefs so as to fully understand the implications of a scenario; and (d) the ability to test ideas and "tentative conclusions" with industry leaders and others, whether or not they were involved in the generation of the framework.

The point of being rigorous about foresight – being strategic – is that it can provide a basis for rethinking the way we do business and repositioning an organization to take advantage of the future before others do so. It's about shaping and creating the Renaissance.

Our experience over many years suggests that leaders need help with this work. Future focused mentoring and coaching for strategic foresight are key components of our work for the last forty years, This is also something we have written extensively about in books, book chapters, logbooks and in presentations around the world.

CHAPTER 7: LEADING SYSTEMATIC CHANGE

In the global knowledge economy, the pace of change is accelerating exponentially, and the challenges are becoming increasingly complex – think climate change, international terrorism, global food security and pandemics. The odds are that a Renaissance Leader will be regularly engaged in leading change – and that more often than in any other period in history, this will mean helping organizations make fundamental changes to what they do and how they operate.

The problem, as David Nadler has pointed out, is that today's organizations have been designed specifically for stability, to provide a buffer from changes in the outside world. Noting how Bismarck's small World War I German army – that had learned much from Max Weber's invention in the late 19th century of "bureaucracy," with its attendant standard procedures, rules, roles, and lines of communication – managed to outmaneuver the "sprawling feudal Russian army," he argues that asking 20th century organizations to change is:

> ...kind of like taking draft horses that were bred, one generation after another, to pull heavy loads and then demanding to know why they can't win the Kentucky Derby. The organizational design most of us have grown up with is just as much a product of natural selection – and it was bred to resist change (p. 307).

Exacerbating the problem is the fact that the Industrial Era mentality encourages taking things apart to find the one piece that needs to be fixed. Organizations looking for a saviour in the latest change fad – be it process re-engineering or teambuilding in the wilderness – will inevitably be disappointed, because they tend to focus on fragmented, one-off actions. They ignore the "web of relationships that make up the organization."

Organizations as congruent systems

In the mid1970s, Nadler, then a professor at Columbia University, became intrigued by work in the physical sciences on systems. It's a simple enough concept: a system as a set of elements that takes input from the environment, subjects it to some form of transformation, produces an output – and the most interesting facet – has the capacity to alter both input and transformation processes based on how output was received or responded to, in other words using feedback to change.

Nadler, his colleague Michael Tushman, and others at Stanford and MIT following parallel tracks began examining businesses through the lens of systems thinking. The result, for Nadler, was the creation of the "congruence model," that has been the foundation of a successful career helping CEOs lead change. The congruence model describes an organization as a system that takes input (in the form of everything that's happening in its environment, the resources both human and material available to it, and the past events and crises that have shaped it), then makes a set of decisions on how to configure resources vis-à-vis the demands, opportunities and constraints of the environment within the context of history. This determines the type of transformation process to which the input will be subjected, in order to produce outputs at the system, unit and individual level – products, services, earnings, and employment.

Nadler replaces the traditional picture of the organization as a hierarchical chart of roles and reporting relationships with a systems view that shows the interaction among:

> "The "hardware" of the organization the work to be done and the formal organization of structures, systems, processes grouping people and work and coordinating their activities; and its "software" the skills and dreams and attitudes of the people doing the work, and the informal organization – the culture, values, beliefs, patterns of communication and influences – how things really get done."

> It's called the congruence model, because what matters is "fit" amongst the components. Change one aspect in any of these boxes, and the whole system is out of whack. That's why the concept of integrated

change, change that is constantly thinking about the interplay of every aspect of the organization, is so important.

Suppose for the moment that you could build your own dream car. You might take the styling of a Jaguar, the power plant of a Porsche, the suspension of a BMW, and the interior of a Rolls-Royce. Put them together and what have you got? Nothing. Why? Because they weren't designed to go together. They don't fit."

— Noted systems theorist Russell Ackoff, quoted in Nadler, (p. 27).

While the model looks very static and left-brain in two dimensions, in application it's highly dynamic. Says Nadler:

> ...it's important to view the congruence model as a tool for organizing your thinking about any organizational situation, rather than as a rigid template you can use to dissect, classify and compartmentalize what you observe. It's a way to make sense out of a constantly changing kaleidoscope of information and impressions — a way to think about organizations as movies rather than snapshots.... Your challenge is to digest and interpret the constant flow of pictures — the relationships, the interactions, the feedback loops — all the elements that make an organization a living organism (p. 43).

Systems thinking as the "fifth discipline"

Peter Senge was a student at MIT at the time Nadler and others were first beginning to think this way. He was fascinated to find business leaders visiting the science department there to learn about systems thinking. Over the years, he has come to regard systems thinking as an important antidote to the "sense of helplessness that many feel as we enter 'the age of interdependence'," overwhelmed by complexity and more information than we can possibly absorb:

Systems thinking is a discipline for seeing wholes. It is a framework for seeing interrelationships rather than things, for seeing patterns of change rather than static "snapshots" .... It is also a set of specific tools and techniques, originating in two threads: in "feedback" concepts of cybernetics and in "servomechanism" engineering theory dating back to the 19th century. During the last thirty years, these tools have been applied to understand a wide range of corporate, urban, regional, economic, political, ecological, and even physiological systems" (p. 68).

Senge's personal contribution in this arena has been helping leaders shift their mindset "from seeing ourselves as separate from the world to connected to the world, from seeing problems as caused by someone or something 'out there' to seeing how our own actions create the problems we experience (pp. 1213)." He helps leaders recognize the simple, archetypal patterns that underlie complex situations (all the more difficult to do because we are part of the pattern) determine what systemic change has the highest leverage, and lead that change in the organization.

Lessons from the New Sciences

Margaret Wheatley, the social anthropologist, suggests we are only in the very early stages of understanding what science can teach us about systems thinking and how it applies to organizations and leadership. If the 20th century organization was designed using assumptions from 17th century Newtonian images of the universe — largely machine based and focused on dissecting the parts — what can the 21st century organization learn from the new sciences of quantum physics, self-organizing systems and chaos theory?

In the early 1990s, Wheatley set out on a journey to explore such questions as: "Why do so many organizations feel dead? Why do projects take so long, develop ever-greater complexity, yet so often fail to achieve any truly significant results? Why does progress, when it appears, so often come from unexpected places, or as a result of surprises or serendipitous events that our planning had not considered? (p. 1)" Immersing herself in the "new sciences," she discovered a new world:

> ...where order and change, autonomy and control were not the great opposites that we had thought them to be. It was a world where change and constant creation signaled new ways of maintaining order and structure. I was reading of chaos that contained order; of information as the primal, creative force; of systems that, by design, fell apart so they could renew themselves; and of invisible forces that structured space and held complex things together (pp. 1-2).

In 1992's Leadership and the New Sciences, she felt she was just beginning to apply these understandings to her work helping organizations change and be effective – looking for patterns of movement over time rather than analyzing parts to death, focusing on structures that might facilitate relationships rather than detailed planning and analysis. This is also when she encountered and explored complexity theory and the way in which it helped us understand the choices that people and organizations made.

Collaboration as the DNA of high-performing organizations

Systems are fundamentally about relationships. Systemic change involves constantly getting all interdependent and moving parts into a proper relationship with the environment and each other to foster organizational health. It's no wonder, then, that organizations are increasingly interested in collaboration – which the Innovation Expedition considers the very DNA of the high performing organization in the knowledge economy. With information technology making it possible to keep geographically dispersed people connected and productive, the role of networks as the soft infrastructure bringing together the expertise to solve complex problems and lead systemic change is coming to the fore.

CHAPTER 8: DRIVING PERFORMANCE WITH PASSION

We have characterized Renaissance Leadership as a particular way of looking at and understanding the world, as a mindset, a way of thinking/doing/being. Renaissance Leadership is equally about delivering results. Renaissance Leaders care deeply about making the world a better place and have a passionate focus on performance at all levels – individual, team, organization. Their goals are as diverse as their interests. They seek to create profitable organizations that are also socially responsible and sought after by employees as wonderful places to work. They strive to build sustainable prosperity in communities: jobs, wealth creation, people oriented social services, a vibrant arts and culture sector, quality of life. They are committed to halting environmental degradation and climate change. They want to do away with poverty and injustice and eliminate global inequity.

Setting the tone

Renaissance Leaders set the tone for organizational performance by talking about their personal goals in concrete terms – terms that reflect the desired outcomes, not just a checklist of activities. They share with their teams the high expectations they have of themselves and how these connect to the larger organizational purpose. They describe how they do regular check-ins with themselves or a coach on whether they're performing at a level that reflects their full capability. They are concrete and clear about the collective results the team is driving toward, and how they're going to get there. We suggest that in a high performing organization in the global knowledge economy, there is much talk about:

> • **Innovation:** The fact that in times of fundamental change, it is the innovators who survive and thrive. That innovation occurs at the individual, organizational, and interorganizational levels, and can take the form of technological or social change. It can involve a product, a process, a business model, an organizational structure, a strategy or a system. Innovation is

a discipline that can be learned

- **Collaboration:** That innovation usually results from collaborative efforts – collaboration within the organization, but especially with outside parties such as suppliers, customers, competitors. That networks provide a collaborative structure to bring together all the expertise required to turn a good idea into reality quickly and efficiently – without the cost in both money and time of creating a complex formal structure, and without constraints of geography

- **Learning:** That the ability to gather, create and integrate new knowledge quickly is a source of competitive advantage. That getting better at learning from experience and sharing knowledge across the organization is critical. That learning is more than keeping up with developments in one's specialized field. It's about an intense and wide-ranging curiosity, an openness to ideas that seem incredible, a desire to seek and use feedback

- **Integrity:** That great performance is driven by a compelling purpose. That the organization has a set of values that inform every decision, every action, and every conversation. It is clear on its social responsibility and how it will live up to it

- **Focus:** That activity for the sake of activity is just wasting energy. That before launching into a task, every individual must understand how that task connects to the larger purpose and strategy of the organization, and why this task takes priority over other possible uses of valuable time

- **Humour:** That fun and laughter are not only allowed but essential. That in a world of uncertainty, the keys to success include flexibility, spontaneity, unconventionality, shrewdness, playfulness, and humility.

Mapping the destination

We believe that improving the productivity of knowledge workers is the central task of Renaissance Leaders in a global, knowledge economy. A chronic challenge is measuring the return on investments made in people and associated costs, physical infrastructure, technology – especially when the output is a knowledge product or a service rather than a tangible thing. It's rarely easy to make a direct link between a single output and a broader outcome, which is impacted by multiple variables. As a fallback position, organizations tend to focus on measuring the amount of activity generated: numbers of meetings, reports, workshops. This makes it very easy for people to become consumed in unproductive "busy work."

Outcome maps and logic models are useful tools for getting leadership teams aligned on the business case for proposed work, for giving employees or team members a holistic view of what they're working toward, and for creating a performance measurement framework. An outcome map identifies business outcomes that align with and support an organization's strategic objectives, as well as the actions required to achieve them. It serves as a "roadmap" for turning strategy into action, and a framework for building a clear logic model and a customized balanced scorecard for tracking performance.

A logic model captures as simply as possible on one page the complex story of:

- Why you're doing what you're doing (challenges, issues, drivers, opportunities)

- What you're investing (resources)

- What you're actually doing (activities)

- What's produced as a result (outputs)

- What changes as a result (outcomes)

Renaissance Leaders develop the ability to use outcome maps and logic models as the "inner voice" of their journey to high performance. They can articulate the logic of their journey at any time – it is their map. Some have such models on display, some use them as a basis for dialogue with their colleagues, and others simply understand this logic.

Measuring progress

The logic model describes the destination; now you need a way of measuring progress towards it. In developing the concept of a balanced scorecard, R. Kaplan and D. Norton of the Harvard Business School were underscoring the point that it is not sufficient to track the traditional financial metrics. Measures of revenue and earnings are backward-looking, capturing the company's success in the last quarter or year, and not necessarily predictive of future success. While share price in theory includes a forward-looking element (investors bet on the company's future success), dramatic swings in the market highlight just how tenuous this link can be in reality.

Throughout the 90s, large corporations were reminded of what proprietors of local "mom-and-pop shops" know all too well— that customer satisfaction, loyalty, and perception of value are the key to sustained revenue and profit growth. They began to recognize and measure how employee engagement/commitment and internal business processes contributed to customer satisfaction and shareholder value. The concept of a balanced scorecard took hold.

While the classic balanced scorecard model is a useful beginning, its power is in starting a conversation within an organization as to what measures will be meaningful in its specific context. This is true in companies, not-for-profits, or public sector organizations. In a not-for-profit, for example, "shareholder value" prompts a discussion of appropriate measures of funder/donor satisfaction or intent to continue to contribute. In many organizations, new categories of measures such as community impact or corporate social responsibility quickly emerge.

For each category on their scorecard, we urge organizations to choose no more than one or two key metrics for the purposes of broad-based communication within the organization and to external stakeholders. While in many organizations there will be a need to track much more detailed management information to keep on course, the purpose of the balanced scorecard is to give a snapshot view of organizational health and ability to sustain performance. If it becomes overly complicated, it's less useful as a tool to engage stakeholders in conversations around organizational performance.

It is also possible for individuals in the organization to have their own balanced scorecards – the measures they need to achieve for their team to be successful. In one organization in which we worked, taking measurement down to the level of the person helped to transform mediocre performance into industry leadership in eight months.

When we worked with Textron – a major US-based international manufacturer – we encountered an organization with high potential for significant improvement. Rather than measure everything that moved, we encouraged Textron to focus on just eight indictors of high performance and by doing so, achieved significant improvements in performance in a short period. Reducing the "noise" of management and sharpening the focus, produced results. This is also what we were able to do for Debenham's (UK), Tesco (UK and Europe) and, more recently, for REACH Edmonton (Edmonton's Council for Safe Communities). The golden rule of this work is that less is more – focus is everything.

The Journey to High Performance

Renaissance Leaders understand what it takes to achieve high performance. Our journey to date has focused on six core elements of their psyche that shape how they view and act in the world. But these six only begin to describe the challenges facing leaders of high performing organizations. In our experience, such leaders:

- Have a vision and set of values that shape their work
- Have a clear strategy which does not change significantly over long periods of time — it is about the "rules" of the game and how the organization wishes to differentiate itself in the market
- Adapt quickly to changing market conditions and opportunities without losing their core values and integrity
- Recruit excellent people, invest in their development (building intellectual capital), and use appropriate methods to capture their knowledge
- Are rigorous about their internal processes and how their structure works
- Focus on speed, efficiency, and effectiveness
- Are outstanding in the way they work with their customers to build commitment and loyalty
- Understand the links among employee engagement ⇒ customer loyalty ⇒ profitability ⇒ shareholder value, and manage these linkages effectively
- Are recognized as developing a best place to work and a best place with which to do business in the industry in which they operate
- Set themselves challenging goals which they frequently achieve — stretching the organization beyond what many think it is capable of
- Make mistakes because they take risks so as to be outstanding, and learn from these mistakes
- Engage and empower their people because they know the organization is focused and aligned around what has to be done
- Embrace constant change as a key to the fabric of the organization, and pursue change with the same rigour they would use for the management of any project
- Embrace technology as a vehicle for improving the performance of the people and systems in which they have invested
- Measure the right things often, but don't let measurement get in the way of performance
- Understand that profitability follows the effective use of all forms of organizational capital — intellectual capital, structural capital and customer capital — not the other way
- *round. By allowing profits to flow, they focus and align the organization on what matters most*

- Make decisions in real time and use time wisely to build the competency to make decisions at the right level throughout the organization
- Are effective and powerful communicators both inside the organization and with their customers and stakeholders
- Manage their supply chain (inbound and outbound logistics) effectively and partner with those in that chain to help improve their performance
- Create powerful and effective communities of customers and communicate with them with integrity, imagination and directness – developing customer loyalty
- Are perceptive and innovative, exhibiting grace under pressure, and departing from convention to achieve their vision without compromising the core values of the organization or their own integrity as leaders.

Each of these is a significant challenge requiring strong, focused leadership. Renaissance Leaders have confidence in their ability to take on such challenges but are also modest about their role in the organization and able to laugh at their own performance. They take their challenge seriously and themselves less so.

CHAPTER 9: DEMONSTRATE COURAGE

We added two additional features of the Renaissance Leadership model as we observed the pandemic and expanded our understanding. The two were: (a) demonstrating courage; and (b) instinctively using Ubuntu as a powerful way of being as a Renaissance leader. We did so, since our connections with leaders struggling to make sense of both the challenges and opportunities the pandemic and its aftermath gave rise to suggested that these two additional leadership characteristics were key to unlocking the potential in organizations, especially post-pandemic.

Types of Courage

Courage is a complex topic, explored more fully in Stephen Murgatroyd's (2023) book *Becoming Courageous – The Skills of Courage*. There are several types of courage Renaissance Leaders will be called upon to display during their leadership career:

Moral Courage

Leaders who put principles first and stand up for what's right, even at personal cost. For example, Fred Keller at Cascade Engineering demonstrated moral courage by implementing a welfare-to-career program in low-income areas of Grand Rapids, showing that for-profit businesses could address social issues while remaining successful.

Speaking-Up Courage

The willingness to voice dissent and challenge groupthink. Peter Weaver, a marketing director, showed speaking-up courage when he openly disagreed with his company president's decision to cut spaghetti sauce prices at a well-known global food manufacturer, instead advocating for product variety and increased advertising. His stance proved correct, while other executives admitted they lacked the courage to speak up.

Innovation Courage

The willingness to take calculated risks and embrace potential failure. Tony, who runs an automotive dealership, demonstrated innovation courage during COVID-19 by completely restructuring his business operations and maintaining his full workforce, which led to increased market share and stronger team culture. In his region, he is the number one automotive retailer.

Crisis Leadership Courage

The ability to make tough decisions during challenging times. Ernest Shackleton exemplified crisis leadership courage through his Antarctic expedition, where he prioritized team morale and cohesion over other resources. It was 1914. The ice trapped and then crushed his ship, *The Endurance*, forcing months of camping on the ice followed by a six-day open boat trip. Next came a truly incredible three-week ordeal as Shackleton and a crew of 5 others crossed 830 miles through hurricane and gale-roiled seas in a modified lifeboat. Then, he and two others traversed the uncharted interior of South Georgia Island (a first) and its perilous combination of mountains and ice fields (32 miles in about 36 hours). Shackleton's multiple attempts to rescue those left behind culminated in his arriving with a rescue ship four months after his departure. Reportedly, he could not bear to watch from the rescue launch as his boatmates counted the number of survivors visible and waving on shore. Everyone had survived. successfully keeping his entire crew alive through very extreme conditions.

Cultural Transformation Courage

The willingness to challenge and change established organizational patterns. Yvon Chouinard, Patagonia's founder, showed transformational courage by creating one of the world's most responsible corporations, demonstrating that doing good and running a successful business aren't mutually exclusive.

Accountability Courage

Taking responsibility for mistakes and being willing to admit errors. Dave is the President of a prominent homebuilding company. Well-entrenched and respected in their market, Dave's company has seen consistent results and success in their 40-year history. They have a young and dynamic leadership team and a great strategic focus that has allowed them to optimize their efficiency. They have adopted leading edge design, pre-build and prefabricated construction for mid and high-end homes. When the pandemic hit, Dave laid off key staff both in leadership and in the construction workforce. Dave soon realized that in making these layoff decisions, his selection process did not account for those people who truly wanted to be there. Some of the people he let go represented the foundational cultural fabric of the company. The team that was left was highly skilled but lacked in their ability to engage with the organization on a value-driven level. He had lost the "core culture" of his very successful business. He has openly acknowledged his mistake and is now working to rebuild the culture and strengthen employee engagement.

The Courage Not to Act

When a leader chooses not to act, when many around them are asking for action. Churchill once said that "courage is what it takes to stand up and speak, it is also what it takes to sit down and listen!" President Kennedy, for example, was being urged to take drastic nuclear action against Russia during the Cuban missile crisis of October 1962, but he chose not to act. Not only did he want to avoid the (estimated) 200 million casualties bombing Russia might involve on both sides, but he wanted to find a more peaceful "way out" of the crisis. As history shows, he was right. Khrushchev pulled back at the last minute, and war was avoided. Kennedy imposed a blockade and sanctions, and he did push exceptionally focused diplomatic efforts to end the crisis, but he chose not to act on the advice of his military leaders.

The Courage to be Vulnerable

When a leader's action makes them vulnerable to criticism or failure. The CEO of Culture Amp demonstrates courageous vulnerability through a unique onboarding ritual. During new employee meetings, he reads W.B. Yeats' poem "The Cloths of Heaven" to each new hire, emphasizing the lines "I have spread my dreams under your feet; Tread softly because you tread on my dreams." This act serves multiple purposes:

1. It shows personal vulnerability by sharing something deeply meaningful to him.

2. It sets an organizational tone encouraging others to bring their whole selves to work daily.

3. It demonstrates that even the CEO is willing to be authentic and emotionally open.

Learning from Failure

Renaissance Leaders will, if they are pushing boundaries and seeking to lead a high performing organization, will fail from time to time. Our late friend and colleague, Don Skilling, was fond of saying "failure is inevitable – learning from failure is an option!" It is the option Renaissance Leaders take every time.

In "Becoming Courageous," Stephen Murgatroyd lists thirteen ways in which failure can trigger learning.

Failure teaches us that success is never guaranteed. You are only as good as your last performance. Just ask anyone born into wealth or born into a company – they will learn the hard way that genetics is not a guarantee of success.

1. **Failure teaches you to embrace change.** Becoming agile, responsive, and nimble is key to moving past a failure to the next success.

2. **Failure can be a great source of motivation.** My failure to secure needed "O" levels in my UK high school – needed (in theory) to be able to stay at school to complete the UK's final two school years, known as Sixth   Form - motivated me more than any success would have done. I ended up securing distinctions and university admission but had to use my political connections (I was a constituency secretary of the governing Labour Party at age 16 – we had control of the Education Committee) to get to stay in school.

3. **Failure may seem final, but it is rarely so.** There are few mistakes, errors or failures that lead to the end of careers, end of hope or end of possibilities. In fact, the failures we made in our work launching the world's first online MBA – a failed offering a certificate in training, a failed summer school – were all moments of truth from which we could build back better.

4. **Failure both broadens and deepens understanding of what it takes to be successful.** This is essentially what both James Dyson and Eddison were saying – having been through so many iterations

60

and made so many mistakes, they had a better understanding of both the nature of success and the conditions necessary to make success possible.

5. **Failure reminds us about humility and its place in success.** One minute you are riding here on the prospect of success and the next you feel down and out. At that moment, humility plays a big part in life. "If it was worth doing, it was worth doing badly" (G.K. Chesterton). Many successful people have failures in their closets (or briefcases or accounts), and their humility comes from these moments.

6. **Failure tells us that not all good ideas are worth pursuing. The idea that just failed was a "great idea" once.** Not all great ideas are as great as we once thought – in fact, some look odd or even ridiculous looking back. A failure helps us improve our ability to determine the difference between an interesting idea and one that is worth pursuing.

7. **Failure reminds us of who is important to us and how important compassion and kindness are.** Failure helps us to see who our friends are and who matters to us. Who shows kindness, compassion, empathy, warmth, and genuineness?

8. **Failure is a test of our ability to manage emotions and our sense of self.** We have a great deal of our "selves" tied up in what we do. When something we were doing fails, then a piece of our "self" is exposed, and we are vulnerable. This requires us to manage our responses, both intellectual and emotional, and learn.

9. **Failure provides an opportunity to reimagine the future and to set new challenges and goals.** Since the future isn't a straight line from the past, failure suggests new directions and opportunities. Spend time reimagining the future, having just learned the lesson Niels Bohr shared: "Prediction is very difficult, especially if it involves the future."

10. **Failure reminds us to eat the frog!** Mark Twain once said that "*If it's your job to eat a frog, it's best to do it first thing in the morning.*

And If it's your job to eat two frogs, it's best to eat the biggest one first." He meant that you should tackle your biggest, most impactful activity first in the day. Just do it; get on with it.

11. **Failure reminds us to pick ourselves up and learn from our mistakes systematically.** Giving up is not an option.

12. **Failure is not fatal – others do not hold failure against you as much as you might think.** In fact, in some places it is welcome. Once you make it clear what you have learned and see new ways of tackling a challenge, others may be more willing to support you now that you have at least one failure under your belt.

13. **Failure shapes courage.** It shows real courage to start again and to connect, build and re-imagine.

Each courageous person we have described used one or more of these responses to their initial challenges and setbacks. Some used several. The point is simple: learning from failure – getting back up again and carrying on – takes courage.

References

Murgatroyd, S. (2023) *Becoming Courageous – The Skills of Courage.* New York: *FutureTHINK* Press | Lulu.

CHAPTER 10: PRACTICE AND LIVE UBUNTU

As we indicated above, the term "ubuntu" is an African term for the idea that strength and capacity derive from connections and collaboration — from the collective — rather than the individual. The underlying idea is that each of us develops our strengths and capacities through connections with others "I am because we are."

Ubuntu is a leadership philosophy in its own right. In Xhosa, Ubuntu means 'humanity toward others', emphasizing interconnectedness, respect and the importance of community. Mutwarasibo and Iken (2019) describe Ubuntu leadership as a way of leading that prioritizes the well-being of all stakeholders and creates a sense of community and belonging. Many leaders are adopting the Ubuntu leadership philosophy to create a more inclusive, empathic workplace worldwide. A good introduction to this thinking can be found in Mungi Ngomane's 2020 book *Everyday Ubuntu — Living Together Better the African Way* (Appetite, Random House). Mungi us the granddaughter of the late Archbishop Desmond Tutu and introduced her book to Canadians at a gathering at the Blackhurst Cultural Centre in Toronto.

For ubuntu, relationships are a leadership's key foci. Developing strong relationships with employees, customers and other stakeholders is a high priority in an Ubuntu-led environment. Employee engagement is enhanced when relationships are prioritized, as it creates a sense of belonging and purpose.

Principles of Ubuntu in Renaissance Leadership

At its foundation, Ubuntu leadership encapsulates the ethos of collectivism, recognizing that an individual's growth and well-being are inextricably tied to the welfare of the community. Ubuntu highlights human interconnectedness and social harmony. Ubuntu for Renaissance Leaders, guided by this philosophy, prioritize establishing strong interpersonal relationships that transcend hierarchical boundaries — they create a culture of the commons. The nurturing of such relationships facilitates open communication, trust and a sense of belonging, all of which helps to create a conducive environment for high performance.

Solidarity

Ubuntu leadership values the importance of solidarity, where individuals within the community support one another despite their differences. Solidarity in this context is not just a theoretical concept but a lived experience, where leaders actively develop a sense of unity and interconnectedness. During challenging times, Ubuntu encourages team members to lean on one another for support, creating a safety net that promotes emotional well-being and collective strength. This sense of solidarity enhances the resilience of the community. It reinforces the idea that the success of each individual is intertwined with the success of the whole. By promoting solidarity, Ubuntu Renaissance Leaders cultivate a culture of trust, loyalty and shared sense of purpose.

Survival

Survival in Ubuntu leadership extends beyond mere existence; it involves thriving and flourishing as a collective. Ubuntu Renaissance Leaders recognize that the survival of the community is not guaranteed solely by individual achievements but by the ability of the collective to adapt, innovate and overcome challenges together.

Ubuntu Renaissance Leaders strive towards an environment that encourages continuous learning, adaptability and resilience. They understand that in the ever-changing professional world, survival requires proactive approaches to challenges and ongoing development. This principle is rooted in the understanding that the collective survival of the community depends on the individual and collective capacity to navigate uncertainties and evolve.

Relationships

Ubuntu leadership places relationships at the forefront of its principles. Leaders who embrace Ubuntu actively maintain connections with their team members, providing an atmosphere of inclusivity and mutual support. Relationships enhance cooperation and encourage a feeling of community, thereby reinforcing the perception that employees' contributions are valued.

Empathy

In Ubuntu Renaissance Leadership, empathy is a fundamental principle. Leaders who practice empathy demonstrate a genuine understanding of their employees' needs, concerns and perspectives. This empathetic approach facilitates emotional resonance and promotes a workplace culture where individuals feel acknowledged and supported, contributing to increased employee engagement.

Collaboration

Ubuntu leaders enable collaboration through the dismantling of hierarchical barriers and the encouragement of ideas and skills. By creating an environment that values diverse contributions and promotes collective problem-solving, collaboration becomes an essential driver of employee engagement and high performance.

Respect

In Ubuntu Renaissance Leadership, respect is highly valued. It is more than just a matter of superficial courtesy. Individuals are valued for their inherent worth and embodied in a deep sense of interconnectedness. In the Ubuntu philosophy, respect takes shape through active listening, inclusivity and empathy. Ubuntu Renaissance Leaders actively listen to others, valuing their perspectives and ensuring every voice is heard and respected. Ubuntu leaders prioritize inclusivity, making sure all members of the community or organization feel valued and appreciated, no matter their background.

Moreover, respect within Ubuntu leadership extends to conflict resolution, cultural sensitivity and ethical conduct. Leaders aim to resolve conflicts while preserving all parties' dignity, appreciate and celebrate cultural diversity, and model ethical behaviour through principles of fairness and integrity. Respect is the cornerstone of Ubuntu leadership. This results in a cohesive organizational culture where individuals feel valued.

Modern Applications and Benefits of Ubuntu

In contemporary organizations, ubuntu leadership principles offer several distinct advantages. First, they naturally support diversity and inclusion initiatives by emphasizing the value of all voices and perspectives. Second, they enhance organizational resilience by building strong networks of relationships that can withstand challenges and adapt to change. Third, they promote innovation by creating psychological safety and encouraging collective creativity. Research indicates that organizations implementing ubuntu-style leadership often experience:

- Increased employee engagement and satisfaction

- Higher levels of innovation and creative problem-solving

- Improved organizational resilience

- Stronger stakeholder relationships

- Enhanced adaptive capacity

While ubuntu Renaissance Leadership offers compelling benefits, implementing these principles in traditionally individualistic organizational cultures presents challenges. Leaders must navigate the tension between individual accountability and collective responsibility, developing new metrics for success that value both personal and collective achievements.

References

Mangaliso, M.P. (2001). Building competitive advantage from ubuntu: Management lessons from South Africa. *Academy of Management Executive*, 15(3), 23-33.

Mutwarasibo, F. & Iken, A. (2019) I am because we are – the contribution of the Ubuntu philosophy to intercultural management thinking. *Intercultural Journal: Zeitschrift fur Interkukturelle Studien*, 18 (32), 15-32.

CHAPTER 11: THE SEVEN C'S AND THE WORK OF RENAISSANCE LEADERS

"Hope is not the conviction that something will turn out well. It is the certainty that something is worth doing no matter how it turns out" - Vaclav Havel.

"No one else is coming. It's up to you." - Margaret J. Wheatley

What does a courageous person do? What kind of capabilities do they display? What kind of skills do they have? What do they do that marks them out from others?

In this chapter, we outline the seven capabilities of courageous Renaissance Leaders. Not all display all seven, but many display combinations of each. We explore how each contributes to courage, with a specific emphasis on what this looks like for leaders in organizations and those in the arts and sciences.

These seven capabilities derive from a life-long exploration of leadership, interpersonal psychology, and organizational behaviour. They were originally developed by Don Simpson and have been refined here.

Curiosity
Definition: an authentic interest in all aspects of their environment.

Curiosity is not just about the work or relationships that directly affect us day to day but about things that cut across boundaries and relate to a broad set of interests.

This week, for example, in addition to writing here, we have been involved in exploring the future of agriculture and food, climate change, digital disruption in both education and healthcare systems as well as issues focused on the future of arts organizations and retail.

Even within a single area of interest, such as digital disruption, we have each reached out to people working around the world on this issue to better understand what they think and know about what is happening and what might happen.

The realization of the ways in which ideas move from one sphere of understanding to another – what those studying innovation refer to as the adopt-adapt process – tells us that curiosity about something often leads to real innovation.

Further, curiosity is the bedrock of science. It is about trying to understand why something is what it is or does what it does not for any purpose but just because "I need to know and understand." Marie Curie provides a good example here. She said, "Nothing in life is to be feared. It is only to be understood. Now is the time to understand more so that we may fear less". She won the Nobel Prize for physics in 1903 but remained curious. In 1922, she won the Nobel again, but this time in chemistry.

All these examples of curiosity require courage to create and the courage to be in the moment of experience when creation and understanding occur. It also takes courage to share with others, who are often skeptical, a discovery, a creation and an invention. Ask any artist who has opened an exhibition of their art or a musician whose work is to be performed for the first time: they will use words that speak to courage.

Creativity
Definition: a capacity to think differently and to design new approaches and solutions.

There is the French term "bricolage," which generally means something constructed or created from a diverse range of available things. In 1966, Claude Levi-Strauss introduced a comparison between engineers who follow rules, procedures and formulae when undertaking their work and a *bricoleur* who uses whatever is at hand to solve a problem and get things done. Bricoleur's must be creative when they solve problems.

Recent studies of innovation suggest that organizations which engage and encourage their employees to practice bricolage – making do with what is available but doing so by adapting and using resources in new and creative ways through improvisation and creative prototyping and networking with others to add capacities – are more resilient and adaptive than those who do not.

Creativity comes, from a willingness to expose ourselves to new ways of thinking and being and then having the courage to share our newfound understanding (expressed by art, music, writing, an innovation, a scientific discovery) to others.

Collaboration
Definition: a willingness and belief that working together to co-create solutions and design new opportunities produces better results than working is isolation.

In the knowledge economy and the emerging industry 4.0, collaboration is the key to success and development – it is the DNA of the knowledge economy.

Take something simple like food production. The Ag-Food supply chain is complex, beginning from seeds or a pair of mating animals and ending up on a fork. This supply chain accounts for 10% of the global economy and employs 1.5 billion people. It is complex and can only work through strong collaboration at each linkage point in the chain. When a link is broken, as it has been from time to time during the pandemic, then the chain is disrupted. Increasing the resilience of the chain and its response to events (e.g., pandemics, climate change, port closures, labour shortages) requires high degrees of collaboration.

Responding to a natural disaster – an earthquake in Haiti, floods in Germany and India, bushfires in Australia, forest fires in British Columbia, volcano eruption in the Philippines – requires intense collaboration between rescue workers, medical teams, public officials, community leaders and technology providers. Colleagues and friends at Médecins Sans Frontières (Doctors without Borders) have developed advanced skills and capabilities in collaborative work in response to such events. So too has Engineers without Borders, who engage in social enterprise to improve the social and physical infrastructure after such a disaster. Their volunteers and aid workers show courage and commitment in their determination to make a difference.

Commitment
Definition: an ability to go the extra mile every time and demonstrate resilience, persistence, and commitment to stay the course.

Being willing is one thing. Being committed and engaged is another. In any attempt to make a difference and have real impact commitment and persistence are what matters. Einstein, when asked why he was so successful as a physicist, once said "it's not that I am smart, it's just that I stay with problems longer" – he was committed to finding solutions to the challenges he grappled with in physics. He added, "I think and think for months and years. Ninety-nine times, the conclusion is false. The hundredth time I am right". That is what commitment looks like. This is what we say with Edison and Dyson at the beginning of the book.

Having the courage to persist is what makes the difference here, especially when those around you are telling you to stop.

Courage
Definition: conviction and belief in oneself

When he looked at organizations that went from good to great, the business writer, Jim Collins identified the setting of "big hairy audacious goals" (BHAG's) as one of the characteristics of organizations that made this journey. Setting goals that were in sight but beyond reach turned out to be powerful motivators for the teams within the organization, especially when each team

70

was able to identify the role they could play in enabling the organization as a whole to achieve the BHAG.

In 1990, Walmart set the goal of becoming a $125 billion company by 2000. As we write this, its market capitalization is $413 billion making it the 17th most valuable company in the world. It easily achieved its 2000 goal.

It took courage to do so. In our work with leaders around the world we saw time and time again courageous leaders challenging their teams and organization to "leap" ahead and achieve goals many thought impossible. The courage to persist, to overcome occasional failures and setbacks and to support the brave is a key feature of leadership.

Some challenges do not need to be financial or corporate. Take Kelsey Mitchell. She had been a successful women's soccer player but at aged 23 she took up cycling in 2017. By 2019 she had set the world record in the cycling "flying 200 metres" and in 2021 she won Olympic gold for Canada in this same event. From not owning a cycle to winning a gold medal in four years is quite the achievement. Kelsey, who is from Alberta, said "I challenged myself from the moment I first got on the bike to become an Olympic champion".

The courage comes from both stating the challenge and then persisting with it.

Competence
Definition: the ability to do something successfully or efficiently.

Competence comes through practice and persistence. Being a competent and capable piano player takes daily practice – as someone said recently, even Mozart had to practice.

Some time ago the book *10,000 Hours – You Become What You Practice* by Phyllis Lane and Rodrigo Coelho was popularized by Malcolm Gladwell in his

71

book *Outliers - The Story of Success*. The idea is that you need to spend something like 10,000 hours developing a skill or competence before you become expert at it. While this is not strictly true – some become expert after just 3,000 hours and others can take nearer 20,000 (one of us gave up the violin for this very reason – it looked like it would take closer to 800,000 hours!) – the key is to connect the development of competency to a goal that matters. Kelsey Mitchell's Olympic medal was linked to her developing the speed-cycling skills needed because she had a major goal in mind and was persistent.

The other point to bear in mind here is that there are different levels of competence. Good enough for playing the violin with friends for fun is not the same as good enough to perform the Prokofiev First Violin Concerto with the Concertgebouw Orchestra in Amsterdam. Hence G.K. Chesterton's quip, "if a thing is worth doing, it is worth doing badly!".

One of the funniest men ever to walk on the stage was Gerard Hoffnung. He loved playing the tuba, which he played with limited competence. He formed an orchestra of amateur players who had a variety of skill levels and competencies. They loved music; they played music, they took it very seriously, and they were either average or below average competence. They were fun to watch. (You can hear recordings of them at the *Interplanetary Music Festival* recorded at the Royal Festival Hall in 1958 on YouTube). The enjoyment they got from playing and sharing their experience was about more than their competence: it was about their confidence in becoming more competent the more they practiced and played together.

Deciding to develop a new competence or capability, especially at a later age, takes some courage. Clifford Davidson, an electrical engineer, and former RAF pilot, decided to develop new skills and understanding after his wife died. He studied at the Open University (UK) for a degree in art and art history and creative writing. He was 90 when he began his studies and 93 when he graduated. He is the oldest person ever to secure a degree in the UK. There are several US graduates who were older when they secured their degree (two were 98), and all say that they needed to do this to prove something to themselves. In each case, they showed determination and persistence. It also took some courage to risk the possibility of failure.

Compassion

Definition: A genuine desire to understand, show warmth and empathy. It includes kindness, generosity, and acceptance.

"If you want others to be happy, practice compassion. If you want to be happy, practice compassion." -Dalai Lama

The Dalai Lama sees compassion and the service we provide to others as the basis for happiness and the defining feature of human life. This is what he says:

> "...compassion and affection help the brain to function more smoothly. Secondarily, compassion gives us inner strength; it gives us self-confidence, and that reduces fear, which, in turn, keeps our mind calm. Therefore, compassion has two functions: it causes our brain to function better, and it brings inner strength. These, then, are the causes of happiness."

More significantly, compassion is also about health. There is strong evidence from a variety of studies of nursing and clinical practice that compassion led to a healthier and more sustained recovery from physical and mental illness. Compassion also reduces anxiety before and after surgery. Compassion also has an impact on patient survival.

Part of the point here is also about self-compassion: showing ourselves the same kind of kindness, care and understanding we would give to others. Rather than judging ourselves, ruminating on our imperfections, and being upset about a failure – showing ourselves empathy, understanding and care.

The first step – showing compassion to others – takes courage, according to our friend and colleague, Professor Paul Gilbert, author of *The Compassionate Mind – A New Approach to Life's Challenges.* Reaching out and sharing a piece of our inner self is a difficult thing to do.

The 7 Cs and Renaissance Leadership

Each of these 7Cs link back to courageous Renaissance Leadership either directly or indirectly. But more importantly, the combination of these 7Cs is what distinguishes a courageous leader from others. Imagine a creative, compassionate, curious person who is challenging the organization she leads to reimagine itself post-pandemic. Imagine a leader who is given an opportunity to create a new kind of arts organization and does so through selecting a small, competent team and fostering creative collaboration with others to reimagine and reconfigure how things get done in music, dance, and art in the inner city. All the courageous people you can think of will have displayed several of the 7Cs in securing their place in history. It is what Renaissance leaders do.

References

Levi Strauss, C. (1966) *The Savage Mind*. Chicago: University of Chicago Press.

Witell, L. et.al (2017) A Bricolage Perspective on Service Innovation. *Journal of Business Research*, Volume 79, pp 290-298.

CHAPTER 12: THE CHALLENGE DIALOGUE SYSTEM AS A CORE SKILL SET FOR RENAISSANCE LEADERS

Introduction

In the 1990s, it was becoming increasingly obvious that change was happening at an ever-increasing rate and that the world and its challenges were becoming more complex and ambiguous. Leaders in this environment require a new set of skills and approaches that go beyond traditional training and experience. Don Simpson, Keith Jones, Stephen Murgatroyd and Janice Simpson together with others in the Innovation Expedition developed the Challenge Dialogue System (CDS) to equip leaders with the tools to foster collaboration, unleash innovation, and navigate the complexities of the knowledge economy.

The CDS Process

Central to CDS is the concept of "Challenge Dialogues," structured conversations that bring together diverse stakeholders to co-create solutions to specific, complex challenges. These dialogues provide a safe space for open and honest communication, encouraging participants to share their perspectives, challenge assumptions, and explore new possibilities. They also identify areas of alignment and agreement and areas of concern or disagreement. The power of CDS lies in its structured yet adaptable 8-step framework, which guides participants through a process of:

- **Defining the challenge:** Articulating a clear and shared understanding of the problem or opportunity to be explored. By doing so, both focus and boundaries are created for the conversation.

- **Setting context:** Providing background information and surfacing underlying assumptions. Not all understand the history, complexity or associated concerns about a challenge or opportunity. By setting context, we can secure alignment and understanding or identify areas in need of clarification.

- **Engaging stakeholders:** Identifying and inviting diverse individuals with relevant perspectives and expertise to engage in a challenging and engaging conversation, initially online and occasionally in-person. In this, some of the techniques used in the Delphi process are employed but all can see and are aware of the issues and concerns expressed.

- **Seeking input:** Gathering feedback through various channels, including online platforms and workshops, one on one interviews, focus groups and other approaches. The aim is to secure rich feedback which can help share the dialogue and truly engage stakeholders in a meaningful, thoughtful and challenging dialogue.

- **Synthesizing and integrating:** Analyzing and consolidating feedback to identify key themes and areas of alignment. Using a "What we Heard" document to capture, categorize and analyze responses moves the dialogue forward, identifying new areas of agreement and new issues to be addressed.

- **Coming together for face-to-face dialogue:** Facilitating focused discussions to clarify issues, explore solutions, and make decisions. This facilitated set of conversations seeks to use a safe space to pursue the underlying challenges and issues and seek resolution and confirmation. Building an area of agreement and alignment, these sessions are focused on "what matters most" and "what must be decided" before the next steps can be taken. Sometimes, this leads to another mini dialogue exploring issues unresolved at the face-to-face session.

- **Developing action plans:** Creating concrete steps for implementing the solutions identified and making progress of the challenges remaining (if any).

- **Monitoring and evaluating:** Tracking progress and making adjustments as needed so that "talk" and sharing become actions that lead to specific, tangible change. Unlike some other processes, the aim here is for the dialogue and collaboration to lead to specific actions and consequences. Sometimes, especially in longer versions of this process, outcome maps and plans are developed so that SMART goals can be set and accountability for change secured.

Three Kinds of Challenge Dialogue

This broad description suggests a particular process, but in fact CDS involves several options. These include, but are not limited to:

1. **CDS Rapid Performance Improvement (RPI):** Supporting organizational transformation through ongoing dialogue and collaboration. Often these rapid CDS processes are undertaken in a few weeks rather than over 6-10 months. As an example, one RPI for the government of Alberta asked Deputy Ministers and Assistant Deputy Ministers across government to identify opportunities and concerns for data sharing in 2000, leading to the creation of a central statistics and data unit for all of government. This work led to the award of the Premiers Award for Innovation in the Public Service.

   In the private sector, CDS was used to guide a two-and-a-half-year transformation process in AVCO - a financial services company – that took them from the bottom rung of companies in a global operation to first in customer, employee and shareholder-satisfaction. Akey factor was development of a process and culture to support co-creation of new strategies, products and operating principles which involved all 1,100 employees in the process over ten weeks.

2. **CDS Challenge Dialogues (CDS):** Organizing time-based dialogues focused on addressing specific key challenges. An ongoing example is the work of the Challenge Dialogue team with the Manitoba Protein Industry looking at the future of the food supply chain and seeking to engage all involved from farm to fork.

3. **CDS Building Innovative Networks (NET):** Facilitating the creation and development of collaborative networks to foster innovation. This has happened in so many projects and initiatives, including helping to create an alliance of the major oil sands companies in Alberta to work collaboratively on climate change to bringing together diverse interests and organizations to focus the work of the Forest Products Innovation centre (FP Innovations) from its founding and for the first six years of its operations.

Why CDS Is Widely Liked and Used: The 12 Powers of CDS

Since CDS was launched in the late 1990s it has been widely used and refined, especially Keith Jones and Tom Ogaranko, who operate the Challenge Dialogue System Network which both undertakes challenge dialogues and trains and then certifies CDS practitioners[i]. There are a variety of reasons for both its functionality and its popularity. They include:

1. **Reality Based** - built around the new realities of an economy which is global, highly competitive, fast-changing and knowledge-based.

2. **Oriented to Stretch Goals** - with a strong emphasis on helping leaders bring about **dramatic** improvements in performance.

3. **Just-in-Time** - capable of fast response to a range of priority needs for information, contacts, processes and tools.

4. **Customized** - able to quickly create customized, high quality knowledge products to fit your priority needs.

5. **Global** - bringing a global perspective, including access to best practice examples, to address local, national or international challenges.

6. **Systems Oriented** - built on systems thinking as the language of the knowledge economy.

7. **Collaborative** - recognizing collaboration as the DNA (the critical element for success) in the knowledge economy.

8. **Geared to Action Learning** - with flexible training modules to support action learning linked to real life challenges.

9. **Leadership Oriented** - providing support for Change Leaders committed to operating as collaborative, entrepreneurial innovators.

10. **Backed by Innovative Tools** - able to provide a wide selection of toolkits focused on specific elements of the journey to support collaborative efforts to drive high performance.

11. **Supported by Mentors and Enabling Technologies** - drawing on new information and communication technologies to provide support systems, including mentoring support anywhere, anytime and online.

12. **Highly Disciplined Process** - using the CDS templates and process maps, the process (rapid or otherwise) follows a set of steps with inputs and outputs at each stage. All involved can understand where they are on the journey to change.

Operating Principles for the Effective Deployment of CDS

The core values informing our use of CDS can best be captured in this statement:

"The CDS Network honours diversity as a source of organizational strength and its way of working is built around the core values of trust, relevance, learning, integrity, inspiration, high performance, resourcefulness, resilience, collaboration, courage, creativity, passion and fun."

It is this thinking and the behaviours it inspires which have enabled the powerful use and deployment of CDS in a range of environments, including non-profit organizations, government department and agencies, for profit businesses, professional bodies, network organizations and industry associations. From these experiences come seventeen operating principles which shape how this work gets done:

1. **Clarify Intentions and Context:** Help groups identify their key challenge and set proper context to the challenge in order to elicit commitment.

2. **Engage in Dialogue:** Use the "8 Keys to Productive Dialogue" to encourage dialogue rather than debate. Develop a capacity for nurturing high-level conversations by posing high-level questions.

3. **Nurture Collaboration:** Advocate and become skilled in nurturing collaboration as the DNA – critical element for success – for the knowledge economy and building resilient communities. Apply the "Suggested Rules for the Road for Nurturing Collaboration" as a good place to start.

4. **Structure the Dialogue Conversation:** Utilize a simple framework — the "CDS Communications Template" — for "holding" the conversation and for helping diverse stakeholders establish some basic information for initiating the dialogue then evolving it. This universal template can be used in numerous situations and formats to engage teams in action initiatives while they also develop key skills: active listening, strategic communication, strategic thinking, systems thinking, design thinking, and synthesis and integration.

5. **Embrace the Power of Co-Creation:** Co-creative processes integrate the skills, expertise, and knowledge of diverse team members (including partners and clients) and leverage their individual contributions to dramatically increase the level, quality, and speed of performance.

6. **Set Expectations and Desired Outcomes:** Write down your collective expectations and desired outcomes of an event (e.g., a meeting, a workshop) or a process (e.g., a dialogue) prior to it occurring. This brings greater clarity, shared ownership of results, and faster decision-making.

7. **Facilitate Purposefully:** Recognize the need for a sensitive, activist and results-orientated facilitation focused on helping the group achieve their expected outcomes and stretch goals.

8. **Build Trust:** Recognize the essential role of "trust" in supporting collaboration, co-creation, and improved performance. Model in one's behaviour the key elements for building and accelerating the speed of achieving trust.

9. **Practice Systems Thinking:** Understand and practice systems thinking as the language of the knowledge economy and building resilient communities.

10. **Hone the Skills of Synthesis, Integration, and Strategic Communication**: Develop and apply these unique skills to bring rich and relevant meaning to the often substantial and varied inputs from diverse dialogue participants.

11. **Establish Criteria First Before Making Choices**: Increase team buy-in and performance - take the time to establish criteria for choices, priorities, and decisions before rushing to make them.

12. **Exercise Your Sense of Humour**: Recognize the importance not only of having a sense of humour, but also the sense in humour.

13. **Utilize Diagnostics**: Use diagnostic tools to identify gaps and priority areas that need team attention.

14. **Draw on Imagination and Practice Innovation**: Help people use their imagination — the foundation of innovation to think outside-of-the-box. Innovation is a discipline that can be taught, learned, and practiced. The way we work together either impedes it or supports it leading to dramatic improvements in performance.

15. **Utilize Technologies Appropriately**: Choose and develop the capacity to successfully use information and communication technology (ICT) appropriately to support quick, easy collaborative interactions and workflow among team and group members.

16. **Access Global to Local Intelligence**: Go beyond your immediate circle of perspectives to tap into glocal knowledge and network resources. Important skills to hone include precision searching, assessing quality, capturing, storing and indexing so it can be found again quickly. Dovetail this knowledge to enrich CDS processes and products.

17. **Apply Distinctive Mentoring Processes**: CDS work with clients and partners invariably includes a mix of CDS practitioners and client staff working together and mentoring one another to co-create and advance dialogue processes and products

seamlessly. This "distinctive mentoring" process and relationship is highly personal, extremely dynamic, and driven by the minds, personalities, and hearts of those engaged. There is no "I" nor "them", only "we"; everyone is valued and has value (see the chapter in this book on mentoring).

Mention is made here of various templates and tools, all of which can be found in the multimedia resource centre for CDS which the CDS Network have developed[2].

Next Steps in The Development of CDS – Powering the Future of The Renaissance Way

Through the smart use of technologies, the CDS process can now be streamlined and refined. For example:

- **Key CDS documents** – the critical issues document, for example – can be instantly translated between one hundred languages, making its use across regions and in multinational organizations easier and more cost-effective.

- Audio and video inputs can be both quickly transcribed and summarized using AI tools.

- Complex documents related to the challenge can also be summarized quickly and linked to other resources needed to understand key components of a specific challenge.

- By loading What we Heard documents into an AI engine, short videos or podcasts can be created almost instantly that communicate areas of alignment and areas of concern to all

---

[2] These can be found at
https://www.dropbox.com/scl/fi/umo8baxpfc8ij2g3637zw/CDS-LP-Dashboard-v15-11x17-20241205.pdf?rlkey=16sym55pc6ujwbdo8l4fp6mzp&e=1&st=htyvc5g0&dl=0

stakeholders rapidly.

- Using video conferencing systems like Zoom or Teams, face-to-face meetings can be replaced by virtual meetings and the dialogue that occurs instantly transcribed and summarized.

- Using AI research tools, organizations who have been through similar challenges or issues can be quickly identified and lessons learned from their experience.

The CDS process, especially through the network of certified practitioners and the training program, is constantly being reviewed, revised and reinvigorated. This is why CDS is in demand.

Why CDS is Important for The Renaissance Way

CDS represents a tangible expression of some key features of the Renaissance Way of thinking and working:

- It is focused on innovative change and development – inspiring "the next" for the organization and helping those who use it be leading edge in what they do.

- It requires and fosters deep-learning and collaboration within an organization and between the organization and its stakeholders.

- It is empowering, engaging and enlightening for all who use it – it operates in the spirit of the renaissance.

- It gives voice to those often marginalized in organizational conversations.

- It challenges people to think from outside the box so that they can better understand the box they are in.

- It asks each person to give the gift of trust and to share in a spirit of making a difference – an essential feature of the Renaissance Way.

For these reasons, we see CDS as a flagship process for the work of Renaissance Leaders and a cornerstone feature of the Renaissance Way.

Chapter Notes

[1] For more information about the Challenge Dialogue System™ Network and its work, see https://www.challengedialoguesystem.net/

CHAPTER 13: MENTORING LEADERS

Leadership is a challenging role for anyone, no matter how experienced they are. It can also be a lonely, demanding and fascinating challenge – one uniquely suited to those who demonstrate the capabilities and capacities described in previous chapters and do so through a lens of optimism. Renaissance Leaders are optimistic by nature but also compassionate and relentlessly focused on organizational change aimed at improved performance. Renaissance Leaders, though skilled, need support not just within the organization, but also from outside. They need and ask for mentoring.

Mentoring and Coaching
Some leaders need coaching about specific developments – how to improve project management, how to think about the deployment of new technology, and how to undertake a skills audit. Coaching often focuses on the "how to" and "what to." In contrast, mentoring is focused on more significant questions and issues related to the work of leadership:

- Questions and explorations that stimulate the leaders' curiosity and broaden their understanding.
- Questions that help them explore the possible, probable and preferable futures.
- Questions which help them better understand how to leverage diversity and include in their thinking different perspectives.
- Questions about leading transformative change initiatives and what can be learned by looking at the experience of others.
- Questions about becoming more courageous while maintaining compassion and care for others.
- Questions and explorations about how, as a leader, they can nurture their colleagues and help them grow and develop as leaders.

The work of mentoring is not so much about "passing on" experiences and insights or of an elder sharing wisdom. It is more about a mutual exploration and the development over time of shared understanding through engaged and inspiring conversation. The mentor shares their wisdom and understanding in a spirit of playfulness, joy, and humour, all aimed at helping the leader become more who they are and can become. As Warren Bennis, one of the great thinkers on leadership, once said, "Leadership is about becoming."

The Seven Leadership Principles of Mentoring in The Renaissance Way
Our understanding of leadership is based on the idea that leadership involves a mindset accessible to all, focused on positive personal credibility, and a commitment to supporting transformational change while serving the needs of others. It is demanding work, yet rewarding, especially if informed by a sense of optimism and playfulness, which informs all of our work.

More specifically, the work of mentoring in which we have been engaged for the last forty years involves these seven principles:

1. In a global knowledge economy, leadership development is one of the highest forms of leverage for an individual, an organization, or a nation.
2. Leadership is a way of thinking – a mindset – and a way of being.
3. Leadership attitudes and behaviours are increasingly expected of most people even though they may not be in a formal leadership position. In most organizations in which we work, leadership is everywhere, not just in the C-Suite.
4. While there is a diverse range of roles which individual leaders may play, the critical role for all leaders is to enable change and to leverage the gains from change for the next change that needs to occur. Change is constant, especially in the volatile, uncertain, complex and ambiguous world in which we all now operate.
5. A person's first leadership responsibility is to demonstrate leadership in his or her own life –that is how personal credibility is established. This is why we give emphasis to personal mastery in our leadership framework.
6. Leadership is more about serving others rather than about having authority and power. Indeed, the idea of the leader as a servant and enabler rather than an enforcer and controller informs all of our thinking and is reflected in our inclusion of ubuntu in our leadership framework.

7. Most people have more leadership potential than they either believe they have or are currently displaying. Indeed, many leaders experience "imposter syndrome" at one or more stages of their leadership development, showing uncertainty at being able to rise to the challenge. Yet many overcome this fear of failure (or fear of success) to achieve great things. A key task of the mentor is to trigger and sustain "self-belief" and the courage to be oneself.

These seven principles are derived from our understanding of how leadership within organizations of all kinds has changed over the last forty years. These changes, captured in the burgeoning leadership literature and a range of TED talks and podcasts, suggest these shifts which we leverage in our thinking:

- **Facilitator first:** A shift from viewing successful leaders as a lonely hero at the top of a hierarchy to being more of a group facilitator, servant or steward. They engage, facilitate, encourage, enable, support, challenge and help both individuals and teams grow, always focused on improving performance.
- **Collaboration rules:** Shifting from the idea that a leader leads by commanding and controlling to enabling through collaboration, networking and connecting.
- **Valuing diversity:** Shifting emphasis from a requirement for conformity to a strong new value placed on diversity and inclusion. In multi-generational, multi-cultural and neuro-diverse organizations, conformity will reduce performance while leveraging diversity and ensuring inclusion will increase it.
- **Systems thinking:** Recognizing that understanding systems thinking and complexity theory as the language of the knowledge economy has become key to unlocking the potential of organizations. Rather than thinking about silos of action, understanding the dynamics of interactions within organizations, between the organization and its stakeholders and within the industry it is a part of is critical for an effective future-focused strategy.
- **Social innovation:** A new perspective built on regenerative thinking and renewal, including recognition of the increased social aspects of innovation and awareness of the changing nature of social and professional networks and their importance. In particular, concerns

about the sustainability of the lands in which we all work, live and play, and the ability of organizations to be trusted stewards of the community in which they operate are becoming front-and-centre issues, especially for next-generation employees and colleagues. This, in turn, has given rise to a demand for balanced, integrated scorecards for measuring outcomes and social contribution.

An implicit understanding, built on twenty-five years of systematic research by the Edelman Group[3], is that organizational leaders (whether in business or non-profits) are amongst the most trusted sources of information and foresight in their communities. Significantly greater trust is extended to such leaders than to journalists, social media, news media or governments. This carries a significant implication for the work of leadership: given that the community has given them the gift of trust, how are they to use that gift in positive and productive ways?

The Focus for Mentoring
Part of the work of the mentor is to help develop leaders' courage, strategic foresight, and personal skills that enable trust to be exercised in powerful ways to bring about change. Sometimes, the work will focus on the leader as a person and sometimes on the challenges they sense in navigating the flow of uncertainty. Most often, the work focuses on possibilities.

Over the last thirty years, our experience suggests that the changing realities faced by leaders require them to explore these things:

- How can I help the organization I lead become more agile and flexible -one that can change direction and strategy quickly as our circumstances change? What can I do to make rapid but strategic responses possible?
- How can I enable more people throughout the organization to feel that they have the authority to act when called upon to do so and to build momentum around the idea of shared responsibility? How do I

---

[3] See more of this work at https://www.edelman.com/trust/trust-barometer

stop people from delegating up and help them recognize the power and importance of their own decision-making?

- How can I enable innovation and real leap-frog change using ad hoc cross-functional teams, which act as skunkworks – responding to a specific challenge and then disbanding until needed again?
- How do I create a learning organization with the capacity to constantly reinvent itself in order to thrive, grow and develop?
- How do I facilitate and develop the different kinds of enabling, and guiding support relationships between senior leaders and their colleagues which learning organizations require?
- How do I frequently refocus the work of leadership on what matters most right now while keeping an eye on what will matter five years from now? How do I strengthen the capacity of leaders to anticipate the future?
- How do I achieve all I need to achieve while living a full and rich life outside of work – achieving a work-life balance which enriches me as a person and gives me the energy to lead effectively?

The Attributes of The Renaissance Way Mentors
Exploring these (and the related questions they each trigger) is the work of the mentor. It is more of an art than a science, more of an expedition than a set of defined and specific practices. The mentor and mentee learn their way to their future together. What the mentor brings to this is both their wide-ranging experience of different organizations, challenges, and possibilities, as well as their philosophy of being and becoming. They bring wisdom, courage, insight and a sense of optimism.

We see nine key attributes and competencies in those who practice Renaissance Way mentoring:

1. They each have a high level of awareness of how to gather, organize, utilize and share resources, ideas, knowledge and skills. They share openly and in the spirit of sharing, rather like craftsmen sharing their ways of understanding and working.

2. They often challenge and question and, in doing so, build confidence.
3. They demonstrate the ability to nurture group dialogues aimed at seeking clarification as opposed to raising criticism and identifying weaknesses. They know how to facilitate a positive, meaningful and fruitful challenge dialogue.
4. They have a natural instinct for active listening and offering authentic feedback.
5. They have strong pattern recognition skills coupled with an ability to synthesize complex ideas, integrate them into work plans and then communicate them to others with "simplicity, the other side of complexity."
6. They have developed the ability to help both themselves and others to acknowledge and respond to failure and learn from mistakes. They have learned that "failure is inevitable, learning from failure is a must-do, not an option."
7. They have developed a capacity to recognize and acknowledge weaknesses and to use them as starting points for learning and development.
8. They display a strong sense of humour and can see the value of humour when attempting to drive major change. They know how to make humour a sign of optimism and possibility.
9. They have a genuine excitement and energy for seeing others succeed.

This is the thinking that informs the work of mentoring.

The Mentors' Way: 8 Keys to Powerful Mentoring Dialogues
In addition to our own experience, we learned from many others – Mile Pegg, Charles Handy, Peter Drucker, Warren Bennis – all of whom we met and engaged with in conversations about mentoring. Over time, we have identified eight keys to effective mentoring dialogues which have stood the test of time. These are:

- **Key 1: Treat the mentoring dialogue as a journey rather than an event.** This requires a real explicit focus on purpose each time a session begins and for the mentor to maintain momentum, which in turn requires focus and discipline. These are not "chats", these sessions are purposive dialogues intended to have consequences.

- **Key 2: Through an agreed statement of purpose, develop shared understanding.** Both the mentor and mentee need to invest in developing a shared understanding of the challenge to be addressed and its complexity. What is key here is to surface "taken-for-granted assumptions and beliefs" that may get in the way of change. We often follow up with a written summary, on which subsequent sessions can build.

- **Key 3: Learn how to collaborate, co-create and anticipate.** Through trust built through dialogue (helped by humour), the mentor can foster effective collaboration aimed at improving the level of courage, commitment to change and employee engagement for the change effort that is the focus of the conversation. Constantly checking what is working in the mentoring relationship (and identifying what isn't) coupled with the use of some simple dialogue tools (e.g. the futures triangle) can make great progress quickly.

- **Key 4: Embrace Diverse Views and Perspectives.** Mentoring is sometimes a 1:1 experience, but sometimes (in our case often) the mentor works with a leadership team. When this is the case, it is essential that the mentor "calls out" and challenges groupthink and works hard to ensure that different voices are heard and that the team develops the art and skill of listening and actively encouraging diversity. From this diversity will come strength and new possibilities. The mentor also helps each person in the team develop the courage needed to voice concerns and challenge orthodoxy.

- **Key 5: Know when to stop exploring and move to action.** One challenge some mentors have is knowing when to stop exploring and reviewing options and to move to action. It is a key challenge. Renaissance Way mentors tend to encourage a faster move to action, based on a careful analysis of options against a set of success criteria. They also demand that their mentees focus on SMART goals (specific, measurable, achievable, realistic, and time-specific), which challenge the organization to make significant changes rather than just an incremental tweak.

- **Key 6: Make smart use of technology.** This is an age when technology is transforming what we do and how we do it. It is the age of AI and quantum computing. An age of technological change for every industry. There are risks here – moving too fast to embrace yet unproven technologies, being too slow to adapt, and locking into technology before the customers are ready for its deployment and use are some of these dangers. Renaissance Way mentors leverage their network of connections to bring appropriate knowledge and understanding to their mentees and challenge them to think carefully about technology-enabled development and change.

- **Key 7: Understand what success looks and feels like.** In our work on developing the skills of anticipation, we often ask leaders to tell stories of the future of their organization. For example, for one organization, we asked four teams of leaders to write a front-page news story for the UK's The Guardian newspaper about the amazing success of the company five years from now. The story had to contain specific success indicators (numbers) as well as what the success felt like for staff, customers and stakeholders. This was then used as the basis for strategic planning. In another example, we used McKinsey's Three Event Horizon tool to help a leadership team see their future unfold over three distinct time periods. The message here is simple: identify tangible, measurable success indicators and couple them with what achieving these will feel like for all staff, customers and stakeholders.

- **Key 8: Plan to sustain performance gains.** It is a sad fact that most change efforts fail, especially when technology is the driver for change. There are many reasons for this, but the key is the lack of a sustained focus by leaders on driving and sustaining the change over time. The mentor must push the leaders they work with to plan for challenges, issues, and concerns and help them overcome failure. They need to engender a spirit of determination by focusing on the agreed benefits of change and the measures of success. From experience, the underlying mentoring task is often to help leaders overcome the fear of change and focus their thinking on the possibilities which will come from success. Underlying this work is to enable leaders to show grace under pressure and to sustain their courage and commitment to change.

CDS and the Work of the Mentor

The Challenge Dialogue System (CDS^{TM}), to be described more fully in the next chapter, is a tool that has been used around the world in support of mentoring by Renaissance Way team members. It helps to identify areas of alignment and focus on challenges which need to be addressed for an organization or network to move forward. It provides both context and focus for the mentor to help leaders take action and change. When coupled with outcome mapping and the balanced scorecard, it can produce a roadmap for change, which can drive performance improvement. Equally important, CDS fosters and enables deep collaboration within an organization and between one organization and others. It is an essential tool in the mentor's tool kit.

However, the most important tool in the mentor's tool kit is knowledge, experience, compassion, and understanding of the work of leadership. What the mentee wants from a mentor is a compassionate but focused challenge based on the mentor's experience. They want to learn to be more courageous when facing the future. That is the master key to this work.

CHAPTER 14: LIVING THE RENAISSANCE WAY

What do those who commit to the Renaissance Way do each day?

Much depends on where they live and their own network context. But there are six key behaviours that characterize what a Renaissance Way practitioner does.

1. **They Seek to Understand the World**
   The world is a complicated, mess of a place. All sorts of events happen from natural disasters, wars and conflict, disease and illness to shifts in the way people interact.

   A renaissance leader seeks to understand not just what is happening, but why. Rather than take an ideological position, the work of understanding requires the renaissance leader to explore different perspectives. For example, while climate change is real, what we do about it is a very complex issue. Renaissance Leaders go beyond slogan policies and strategies like "net zero by 2030" and look at what more realistic and practical options for change might be. They connect and explore with scientists, policymakers, innovators and entrepreneurs to identify possibilities. As change makers, Renaissance Leaders work to make change and development happen.

2. **They Make and Sustain Connections**
   A key task is to engage and practice cross-boundary learning and to think and act glocally (using global understanding and networks to make a difference locally). To do this, requires Renaissance Leaders to maintain direct and focused connections with colleagues, friends and innovative leaders all over the world.

   Back in the late 1960s, this was called "working the rolodex" – using the business card collection to maintain information about colleagues and build a network. Now we use technologies like email, Zoom, blogs and podcasts to connect.

   In a typical week, one renaissance leader we work with receives and responds to over six hundred emails from colleagues and leaders in twenty countries and reaches out by Zoom or Microsoft Teams to some of them for quick 10–15-minute catch ups.

Some Renaissance Leaders teach graduate students, seeing this work as both sharing understanding, but also constantly expanding this network.

Another is addicted to writing. In 2024, he published two comprehensive books, five book chapters in books edited by different people as well as publishing three articles in journals, magazines or newspapers. Each of these publications expands his connections and network, leads to invitations to speak and work around the world and leads to others wanting to connect with him. He says, "books are just one big business card" – they create an opportunity to connect with others.

3. **They Connect People to Each Other**
   A key role Renaissance Leaders play is to connect individuals or teams to like-minded others. In one week, the coauthors of this book connected an entrepreneur working on a breakthrough technology (a finalist in Prince William's Earthshot Prize) with a creative developer of AR/VR technologies based in Uruguay, an innovative leader in a large national bank with a creative developer of financial services technology, school leaders from Australia with school leaders and innovators in Canada, and a writer seeking to publish a book about sulphur hexafluoride (known as SF_6) with a publisher. Such weeks are not unusual.

In addition to connecting individuals or teams, Renaissance Leaders reach out to make connections possible. In October, one of the authors of this book reached out to five people they admire but did not know: Ethan Mollick (author of Co-Intelligence – Living and Working with AI), Darcy Hardy (a legend in online learning), Phillipa Hardman (author and entrepreneur) and Professor Gert Biesta, one of the leading philosophers of education in the world. All agreed to speak and connect and all shared real insights. If you don't reach and out and ask, the opportunity to connect will not occur. Now that a connection has been made, each of these persons is now connected to others in the Renaissance Way network who may benefit from their knowledge, wisdom and skills.

4. **They Seek to Shift Mindsets**

Mentoring is a key role of Renaissance Way Leaders. They engage with others and help them understand their leadership journey. For example, they help them identify the burden and weight of the past and how it shapes the present and limits the future. They help them understand the present and the context in which they operate and the push of the future. They also help them understand the pull of the future and the ways of anticipation.

We have written extensively on the Renaissance Way approach to mentoring (Murgatroyd 2024a, 2024b), and the logbooks of the innovation expedition and related travel guides explain the approach in more detail. The underlying focus for this work is to build the capacity of leaders to show courage and commitment and to lead change with passion.

5. **They Tell Stories**

Storytelling and using stories as prompts for action and change is a key skill of a renaissance leader. For us, this has been part of the work we have engaged in since the 1960s and 1970s. Stories of change and transformation, stories of failure as a basis for deep-learning, stories of challenge and success, stories of struggle and possibilities, stories of learning – all are part of the rich tapestry of learning resources and departure points for change.

In an early meeting of the Innovation Expedition held at the Banff Centre – the audience was senior business and government leaders from Alberta – we invited a trumpeter from the Calgary Philharmonic Orchestra to talk to the assembled group. He told a wonderful story of preparing for a particular performance of Mahler's 4th Symphony – practising some of the more difficult parts time and time again at home – only to arrive at the concert to find that they were performing Mahler's 5th symphony. A very different piece with very different demands for the trumpet. He had to sight read, pay much more attention to the conductor than he would normally do and pay very close attention to the playing of others in the orchestra. He "muddled through with courage, skill and determination" and, in his view, gave the best performance he had ever given. This story resonated with all in the room, and as we unpacked parallels with the experience of oil and gas executives, government Deputy Ministers, CEOs of small and medium enterprises, we heard versions of similar experiences from all who spoke.

When we launched the leadership program at Conoco Phillips, we asked NHL legend Craig Simpson to talk to our leaders. He described the different ways in which the teams he had played on – the Edmonton Oilers, Pittsburgh Penguins and Buffalo Sabres – welcomed him and the way in which his first two months on each team shaped his feelings and playing. He was making the point that orientation and connection shape attitudes and behaviour from day one.

At a recent event for a major Canadian bank, swimming legend and Olympic gold medal winner Mark Tewksbury shared his experience of building his confidence, skill and determination to win the Olympic Gold medal for the 100-metre backstroke in 1992. He explained that a change of coaching support led to a change in his mindset and his swimming technique. These changes were significant given that the difference between first and second place is measured in hundredths of a second. He explained the implications of his experience for seeking to manage change.

Sharing experiences and understanding through stories is a powerful way of making change and transformation real and tangible. It suggests, "If they can do it, so can you." The key is to keep the story tight and focused and make an initial connection to the people in the room.

6. **They Give the Gift of Trust**

Renaissance Leaders "pay it forward" – sharing their knowledge, understanding, resources and skills with others. For example, a young researcher connected with one of us asked if they could receive some coaching about writing an academic paper for a journal. This led to a shared author paper in a journal in Paraguay between one of us and a scholar in Turkey.

To make this possible, we give the gift of trust. We trust the other person will show respect and use the sharing wisely and trust them to do so. If, for whatever reason, they show disrespect or abuse the trust, then the relationship ends or the issues are confronted so that we can move on. The gift of trust is offered in the spirit of ubuntu — "I am because we are" — and in the spirit of reciprocity. Each of us has benefited from the gift of trust from others and from being mentored and coached by others in the early stages of our careers.

The Underlying Characteristics of a Renaissance Way Leader

When you review these six behaviours of those living The Renaissance Way, three underlying characteristics become apparent. They are:

1. **Curiosity and exploration** — they want to understand and make connections between ideas, development, opportunities and challenges.
2. **Connections and sharing** — they willingly and actively seek out connections that will enrich their understanding or connect them to new ways of working or new challenges and opportunities.
3. **Challenges and the pursuit of possibilities** — they see opportunities and possibilities, sometimes, whereas others just see difficulties and obstacles. Given the richness of their experience and the connections they can bring to bear on a situation, Renaissance Leaders adopt a "can do, let's do" mindset rather than a "looks difficult, let's not" mindset. As Don Simpson often says, "he is a cockeyed optimist in a sea of pessimists."

When taken together, these six activities and three characteristics make life interesting. We often find ourselves at the edge of developments — just this year; an Earthshot prize winner, the use of AI/VR to help young people understand their Indigenous (Cree) history, new developments in AI and leadership, new opportunities for reimagining higher education around the world — all because of these activities.

It is a rich way of being – enriching the lives and work of others.

References

Murgatroyd, S. (2024a). *Mentoring Leaders for Courage*. In Aris, S., Roycroft, P., & Rao, A. (Eds.), Mentoring Handbook – Approaches for Health and Social Care. Shoreham, UK: Pavilion.

Murgatroyd, S. (2024b). *Changing Minds Through Futures-Focused Mentoring*. In Aris, S., Roycroft, P., & Rao, A. (Eds.), Mentoring Handbook – Approaches for Health and Social Care. Shoreham, UK: Pavilion.

CHAPTER 15: THE RENAISSANCE NETWORK AND ITS POTENTIAL

Over the last thirty years, under the conscious guidance of Don Simpson with significant support from Keith Jones, Stephen Murgatroyd, Tom Ogaranko, Brenda Kennedy, Leah Andrew, Carlos Algandona and others, an international network of like-minded individuals have collaborated and engaged in ongoing project work. Such work has ranged from a leadership program for a major oil and gas company or for one of the world's leading pharma companies to the development of a social enterprise centre in Kenya and the taking of decisive action in relation to food waste.

The network is a loose Collaboratory. It is an informal but highly impactful network. Its key features are:

- All members share a set of values and beliefs which connect them in both intellectual and socio-emotional ways.
- All are willing to share their skills, knowledge, and understanding with others in open and creative ways, and they thrive on challenges that utilize their knowledge and skills.
- All have significant experience and expertise, though the range of that expertise varies significantly — artists, doctors, musicians, writers, consultants, filmmakers, technologists, business leaders, non-profit leaders, and senior figures in government.
- All share an understanding of the wicked and complex problems the world is facing but do so from their own lens and perspective. That is, the network is open to those who have different perspectives and views of major issues provided they share a commitment to collaboration and openness in helping organizations deal successfully with complex tasks and thus drive transformational change.
- The network is virtual and, for many, distant — yet is called on from time to time by network colleagues from around the world to support or help with specific challenges or tasks.

When we describe this network, which has occasionally met in person, we are asked many questions. In this short chapter, we seek to answer them.

Frequently Asked Questions About The Renaissance Way Network

1. **How did you manage to start this network 30 years ago?**
We had specific challenges to address – the sustainable future of Alberta's oil and gas sector, forestry and agriculture industries and the challenges of shifting from an "old" top-down hierarchical form of organization to more innovative, agile and creative organizations. We had specific challenges to address and realized that these could not be addressed through "traditional" consulting and educational practices. A new approach was needed.

Through the Banff Centre and Athabasca University, we founded a Collaboratory that enabled like-minded people to collaborate and engage without them having to change their occupations or roles: we leveraged knowledge, skills, understanding and imagination to make things possible.

One specific development – the Challenge Dialogue System (CDS) – also created a formalized mechanism for the exploration of change and development. Now codified (there are formal certification processes and practice designations), CDS has been used extensively in private corporations, government agencies (municipal, State and provincial, Federal), non-profit and charitable organizations and by professional bodies to support their change leadership efforts. This development involved the collaboration of many in the network, some of whom met from time to time.

2. **Who funded the start-up?**
The biggest single factor in starting and sustaining a network is emotional commitment and time. From time to time, money can be helpful – but shared values and communication are the keys. Some "funny money" (small budget amounts) from the Banff Centre, Athabasca University and a portion of net revenue from client-facing

work helped lubricate the start of the network. The rest has been a labour of commitment, courage and care.

Some of the most important networks in history have not been funded by grants or investment. Think of networks like the Suffragettes or the Hospice Movement or the Campaign for Nuclear Disarmament (CND). Fueled by conviction, determination and compassion, these movements had their impact not because of the size of their budget but because of the courage of the members of the network. That is the story here, especially in the early days.

Network colleagues gave work – consulting, mentoring, coaching and challenge dialogue work – to others in the network to meet an organizational need they were responsible for. In doing so, the network grew in terms of both experience and depth of network member relationships. The network of collaborators did not require anyone to change their occupation, roles within existing organizations or to engage in complex legal agreements. We simply agreed to work together.

This work was greatly aided and enabled by the development of the Challenge Dialogue System (CDS), CDS is a powerful organizational improvement system with a proven track record globally. It assists team of diverse stakeholders to mobilize and collaborate in solving complex problems. In doing so, it leads to transformational change.

3. **Why did you make such a commitment to lead and sustain the network over the thirty years?**

At the launch of the network in 1992 – at the Banff Centre, with its focus on nurturing creativity through the arts – we were surrounded by examples of the ways in which artists can add to the broader base of leadership development. We embraced them and integrated artistic understanding and experience in all that we did.

When faced with challenges or opportunities, there are opportunities to partner and co-operate with some like-minded, value-sharing colleagues around the world so as to better meet the needs of clients and colleagues. Sustaining the network enables us to do this. This also enables us to better meet the needs of clients and partner organizations.

For example, when asked to look at the future of animal and human health by a UN organization, we turned to colleagues in Canada, Africa, India and Asia (all part of the network) to help us, meeting in Kenya and the UK to explore the findings of two separate challenge dialogues.

Working on the future of the forest industry in Alberta, we turned to our colleagues in Finland, Sweden, Brazil and Australia to improve and develop our understanding of the dynamics of the forest industry sector. The network provided basic connections which are then leveraged to help provide world-class responses to a social, organizational business or other challenge. We work better together than alone. This work also brings a great deal of personal satisfaction – knowing that you are working to make a difference helps.

The network keeps expanding. We held a gathering of key network members in Toronto under the leadership of Chris Katurna, author of *Age of Discovery – Navigating the Storms of Our Second Renaissance* (with Ian Goldin) – and again in various locations working with Seth Goldenberg author of *Radical Curiosity – Questioning Commonly Held Beliefs to Imagine Flourishing Futures* and found more like-minded colleagues.

More recently, working with the team at ICChange under the leadership of Abdullah Saleh with the focused skills of our colleague Brenda Kennedy, we are cementing the future of the network under the ICChange umbrella.

4. **How did you manage to attract so many high-quality mentors to become part of the network and how are they funded?**

Quality attracts quality. When others read or hear about the work being done by members of the network, whether on business, health, non-profits, sustainable development or the arts, they want to connect. If we see that others are doing imaginative and creative work which

104

is aligned with our values and vision, we will connect with them. It is surprising how, when we do so, most are grateful to find and connect with a like-minded person from Canada.

Indeed, this last month Stephen has been connecting with some of the leading figures working on artificial intelligence for education – he is writing (with his long-time colleague, J-C Couture) a book for a major publisher on this theme. He has spoken with twenty-five leading figures in this space, none of whom he knew. Six are keeping in touch.

Writing helps. We both see books like this one as "big and long" business cards. They provide a depth of understanding of our thinking, and in doing so, reveal who we are and what we stand for. Stephen has over fifty books and over 450 book chapters, academic papers, magazine and journal articles to his name. This has led to global travel to present keynotes and workshops all over the world (most recently in Dubai, New Zealand, Australia, Mauritius, South Africa) – at each such event, a new mentor or colleague is found and added to the network.

5. **Since the beginning, the network has worked with business, community-based organizations and non-profits, arts organizations, sports, public institutions and many other kinds of organizations. What led to this strategy and how did you build the capacity to function in this comprehensive and integrated manner?**

Both Stephen and Don both have strong backgrounds in a range of different kinds of organizations, having volunteered for board and leadership roles in many kinds of voluntary, non-profit and related organizations. Stephen also trained as a therapist and psychologist using systems thinking and systems dynamics. Both realized early in their careers that all organizations are systems and all are essentially the same, though their strategic intentions may differ. All struggle with people issues, with sustaining momentum, with managing change, and with technology.

We also realized that lessons learned in one sphere – say an arts organization struggling to sustain itself – are transferable (with some interpretation and minor adjustment) to another sphere, say a business start-up. We often brought the two together so that key players could share their surprise and delight that, even though the context and intentions are different, their underlying issues were the same. We have been reminding leaders of the powerful role the artistic community played in triggering major changes across many sectors in the iconic European Renaissance, which transformed medieval society into the modern era. Our focus on encouraging similar catalytic actions today has also involved artists and creatives – hence our mantra "an artist at every table."

In working on the arts games – part of the cultural Olympiad – we explored issues of focus, strategy, skills and impact – all issues we had just been exploring in relation to the reinvention of higher education in New Zealand.

The mind-set we use sees organizations as systems, and while each system may have some unique features, these are outnumbered by the systems features they have in common. Understanding this, we were able to quickly transfer mentoring and change management approaches from one sector to another.

This skill was refined during the time we ran Lifeskills International Ltd. in the UK – a high performing consulting company. In a typical week we worked with a bank, one of the largest food retailers in the world, a high street clothing retailer, an arts organization and the BBC. The underlying skills – a focus on people, systems, impact and engagement – were the same, nuanced by the context.

This became exceptionally clear when, under the leadership of Dawn Ralph, we were involved in designing the evaluation process and support systems for the Peter Drucker Award for Canadian Non-Profit Leadership. This required us to codify excellence across the not-for-profit sector, focusing on how innovation and impact could be

106

evaluated. This also helped with a major evaluation of a decade of work of both the International Institute for Sustainable Development and then the Commonwealth of Learning. Models and frameworks, adapted for context, become transferable.

6. **How did you manage to produce such high-quality tools, processes and specialized resources? What granting agencies supported you?**

The work undertaken by the network frequently required the use of facilitation or other tools or resources to enable engaged and inspiring conversations. Whether these tools already existed — e.g. the futures triangle, the Gartner hype curve, McKinsey's three event horizon, scenarios[4] — or we had to invent them. We borrowed with glee and developed new tools to test and try. No funding was sought for these developments, though some revenue from clients was used to support this work.

As an example, we developed a business simulation with several stages for a major event at Textron. It involved teamwork, team collaboration, lots of challenges which were introduced at random. The aim was to reflect day to day operations at Textron, but to do so with humour, fun and challenge. It worked and has been used with several others since.

For our work with forest companies in Alberta, we adapted a tool we had seen used at the Ontario School of Art and Design (now OCAD University) developed by Stuart Candy. We customized A Thing from the Future to meet the needs of the situation. More recently, we adapted an AI simulation developed by Ethan Mollick (author of *Co-Intelligence — Living and Working with AI*) for use with graduate

---

[4] You can explore these and other futures thinking tools in Couture, J-C and Murgatroyd, S. (2024). *Education Futures for School Leadership — Evidence Informed Strategies for Managing Change*. Routledge.

students developing use cases for the deployment of AI in their schools.

The key tools – the Challenge Dialogue System for example – have been developed and codified over time, mainly by Jan Simpson, Keith Jones and Tom Ogaranko with some help from time to time from Don Simpson, Stephen Murgatroyd and others in the network. You can see these tools and the processes associated with them at the Challenge Dialogue System website.

In short, tool kits and resources are created in response to specific needs and then reviewed and adapted for more general use. This "adopt and adapt" approach to the development of tools and resources is a key characteristic of the working method of the Renaissance Way.

What's Next for The Renaissance Way and the Network?

From the end of 2024, Don Simpson (now 90) and Stephen Murgatroyd (a young 74) are stepping away from the day-to-day management and support of the network and moving on.

Don is dedicating himself to bringing his work as a storyteller to life through audio, video, and public performances. His vision is to serve as a travelling, informed ambassador for optimism and hope. Sharing stories of the Renaissance Way and, in doing so, inspiring individuals and organizations to become Renaissance Leaders living the Renaissance Way. A key mantra of his storytelling is his sense that "in troubling times like the ones in which we find ourselves, progressive individuals should see optimism as a sense of duty, not as an indulgence."

Stephen is winding down his teaching and academic work and focusing on writing – three new books and a few novels are in the works, with the most recent books published in May, October and December of 2024.

The Logbooks of the Chief Explorer – a detailed and thorough account of Don's life and work in fourteen volumes (4,000 pages) are now available in the library at Trent University and will soon be available digitally. Travel Guides to key topics captured in this book are also soon to be available digitally. Don's archives are also available at York University.

The future of the network is in the hands of Dr. Brenda Kennedy and Abdullah Saleh of ICChange. Indeed, over time the intention is to merge the work into the non-profit and charitable arms of ICChange and for Don's intellectual property to be available through this organization. ICChange is an organization that deeply reflects all of the values and principles of the Renaissance Way and is led by individuals who fully embrace Renaissance Leadership in all of its aspects.

Five Challenges for the Future

In looking at the journey to date and the future, five major challenges need now to be addressed for those engaged in sustaining and developing The Renaissance Way:

1. **How do we enable more individuals, teams and organizations to engage in the brave and courageous conversations required to make work, community and society better?** This requires developing the skills of active engagement, overcoming barriers to listening to the ideas of others with whom we disagree with but can see value in, and recognizing pathways to possibilities more often than barriers to action. It also means cultivating compassionate, courageous, and determined leadership focused on change and development.

2. **How do we imbue thinking about the future with a sense of beauty and lyricism, with artistic imagination?** While many see science and technology as the key to the future, they are just part of the story. We need to see art, design, music, dance, sculpture, theatre and other

forms of the arts as unlocking the human spirit, enabling healing and encouraging a humanistic view of possibility. We need an artist at every table.

3. **How do we tackle collectively and collaboratively the big issues of our time in imaginative and creative ways?** Challenges like climate change, the future of agriculture and forestry, the restoration of a sense of community, the ability to develop trust in change – how can the Renaissance Way network facilitate the future in ways that help people and communities heal, develop and grow.

4. **How do we forge connections across cultures?** With the world in flux and immigration the key to the developed world's future (especially given the low birth rates and declining fertility seen around the developed world), how can we use the mindset of the Renaissance Way to build bridges, develop the capacity to learn and engage with each other and overcome cultural and social barriers to building a community? Can we use technology (especially instant translation) to help with this work? Can we develop mentoring approaches for those who lead organizations dedicated to this work?

5. **How do we drive performance improvement and impact of the organizations we work with so that they do more and have more impact with the same or fewer resources?** This is core work for all in the network – strengthening the performance, impact and reach of all organizations and maximizing the deployment of the skills and resources available to them. This is the key task the network has been working on for thirty years and the work is not done: there is more to do.

As you look at the five challenges we see for the future of the network and the Renaissance Way, know that there are hundreds, if not thousands, around the world who are working on these questions. The big challenge is to connect them and encourage and enable them to do more together. That is the future network.

"Alone we can do so little. Together we can do so much!"
Helen Keller.